Pain Free

Pain Free

Biblical Methods that will Bring Healing to the Emotional Hurts of Your Past

———

Glenn T. Dorsey

ISBN: 0692838260
ISBN 13: 9780692838266

Unless otherwise indicated, all Scripture is taken from The Holy Bible, English Standard Version. Copyright © 2001 by Crossway Bibles, a division of Good News Publishers.

Scripture marked KJV is taken from the King James Version of the Bible.

Scripture marked NIV is taken from the Holy Bible, New International Version®, NIV® Copyright © 1973, 1978, 1984, 2011 by Biblica, Inc.® Used by permission. All rights reserved worldwide.

Scripture marked NKJV is taken from The Holy Bible, New King James Version. Copyright © 1982 by Thomas Nelson, Inc.

Scripture marked NLT is taken from the Holy Bible. New Living Translation. Copyright © 1996, 2004, 2007, 2013 by Tyndale House Foundation. Used by permission of Tyndale House Publishers Inc., Carol Stream, Illinois 60188. All rights reserved.

Dedication

I want to dedicate this book to two people that have profoundly affected my life.
Their lives are a testimony to the wholeness that comes out of the emotional healing process.

Both of them are on my heroes list because they have overcome many traumas in life and are living the 'Pain Free' life. These two individuals inspired a great deal of this books content.

Dewayne Weeks has been a spiritual son and played the important role of Hur in my life. Julie Ballard has responded to the call of God to take the mantle and message of emotional healing to prisons, rehabs, conferences, and churches. I claim her as a daughter. Thank you both for what you mean to my ministry and my personal life.

Pain Free

Introduction

———◆———

I WAS HAVING A CONVERSATION with a close missionary friend, Dr. Jim Bennett, when he made a statement that I could not get out of my head. He said, "Glenn whenever your body is in pain you need to pay attention to it. It is telling you that something is wrong."

The next day I was in the gym, at a local university, playing basketball with some college students. I began to lose my breath when I would exert myself. It was severe enough that the only way I was able to play would be to sit out for a couple of minutes and get back in the game. I knew I was in good condition and I couldn't understand why I was fatigued so easily.

That night I received a phone call from my mother. She said, "Glenn are you okay? I had a dream last night that you had a heart attack." I laughed and quipped, "Mom, I am fine. You missed it this time." She said, "Well, it was so real I had to call and check on you."

The next day I was bent over inspecting a car I had bought for my daughter when suddenly a severe pain went down my left arm. The previous conversation I had with Dr. Bennett came rushing into my mind. I called my physician and informed him that I thought I was having angina. He instructed me to immediately go to the emergency room.

It was discovered that I had artery blockage. The artery that was blocked is called "the widow maker." It is the main blood supply to the heart. At the age of 39 I had open-heart surgery. The surgeon told me after the surgery if I had delayed getting to the hospital I would not have had a heart attack. Instead, my heart would have exploded.

If I had ignored the pain I would have died.

The pain that I want to address is not just that of the body but also of the soul. Emotional pain like that of the body cannot be ignored. The body and soul are so intertwined that they share pain. One can affect the other. Just as the body has malfunctions that cause pain it is also true of the soul.

We often ignore the pain thinking that it will heal itself. It is obvious that if we do not seek a diagnosis not only will the pain continue, it will worsen.

Jeremiah expresses the frustration that we all have with pain.

Jeremiah 15:18 (ESV)
"Why is my *pain unceasing*, my wound incurable, *refusing to be healed?"*
For some days, I had discomforting back pain. Tests were performed and I had treatments that would ease the pain only temporarily. Instead of resting my back and abstaining from physical activity I continued to be active. That was a tremendous mistake.

While playing golf with my son and a friend, in the middle of my back swing, something slipped in my back. I fell to my knees in excruciating pain. Knowing I could not continue I went immediately to the emergency room. It was discovered that I had a ruptured disc and I was scheduled for back surgery. There was no position I could get in to ease the intense pain. The only method of treatment that would stop the pain was surgery.

To ignore your pain guarantees that it will worsen. This truth applies to our emotional pain. Denial and delay will not allow the pain to lessen. The only cure for pain is to acknowledge it, identify it, seek professional help, and do what you are instructed to do. The goal of this book is to lead you into the pain free life by scriptural truth and application.

CHAPTER 1

Pain Can Produce Gain

———◆———

HUMAN NATURE DESIRES A QUICK cure for pain. We go to the physician and expect him to give us a pill that will bring about a rapid cure or relief. We do not condition ourselves to deal with persistent pain. Yet life will always consist of overcoming some form of pain.

Pain that persists draws out the dross from your faith even as fire separates dross from the gold. **In your suffering, true character is established in your spiritual life.** The people you know who are strongest in faith are those who have endured the fiery trials of life and maintained their testimony. They have learned the value of patience.

Job is a perfect example of a person dealing with extended pain. In all that he suffered God was at work to produce an even greater man than he was before. What kind of man was he before?

Job 1:8 (NKJV)
"Then the Lord said to Satan, 'Have you considered My servant Job, that there is none like him on the earth, a blameless and upright man, one who fears God and shuns evil?'"

According to God's own standard it does not appear that Job needs any improvement. What more could be said about a man than that he is blameless and there is none like him on the earth? God is choosing the best and is going to make him better.

Whatever pain you are dealing with today God is going to use to make you a better person in the future.

When dealing with persistent pain, like Job, we tend to feel that God is far from us. We also may reach a place that we would say I would rather die than live. Job's attitude was, "Though God slay me yet will I trust in him."

What brought an end to Job's suffering? It was when God began to speak to him out of the whirlwind. That whirlwind represents the disturbances in Job's life. God has not abandoned you. He is going to speak to you in the midst of your suffering. When you hear His voice it is a clear indication of His presence. It is a fact that we can go through anything in life if we know that God is with us.

Whatever you are experiencing it is not just about you. God is going to use your painful life experience to bring healing to others who are experiencing similar life struggles.

You can make the mistake of attempting to remove all pain and discomfort from your children. It will work against their future development. Children need you to guide their response to pain. Teach them that pain is just temporary but can have long-term benefits. Share with them stories of how God used pain and turned it into personal strength.

Job is instructed by God to pray for his friends who accused him of sin. When he did, God restored double what he had lost.

Your attitude determines how quickly you will be healed. You can isolate yourself, have a pity party, and experience no personal growth. On the other hand, you can choose to trust God and know that nothing that is happening in your life is coincidental or accidental. We know that God is working all things together for our good.

WHAT IS THE PURPOSE OF PAIN?

Pain is an alarm system to the body or soul that something is not right. Its purpose is to put you on a path to bring healing and change.

Are you suffering from physical or emotional pain? Have medical tests been made but no cause for the pain is discovered? It may be rooted in an emotion, which is stressing the body.

Americans spend twice as much on health care per capita as any other country in the world. According to a series of studies by the consulting firm McKinsey & Co., the U.S. spends more on health care than the next 10 biggest spenders *combined*: Japan, Germany, France, China, the U.K., Italy, Canada, Brazil, Spain, and Australia.

Over 100 million Americans suffer from pain. The estimated cost to society is between $500 and $635 billion annually. Much of this medical treatment is related to pain. Of course, there are legitimate reasons for pain such as accidents, infection, etc. Yet after tests are made with the finest of medical equipment, the source or cause of the pain still remains undiscovered. This leads to an obvious conclusion that the pain is perhaps being caused by emotional stress or is spiritually related.

God's Word is life and spirit. Like a surgeon's scalpel it has the power to divide the soul and the spirit. The soul is your mind, will, and emotions. **Your health is affected by the health of your soul.**

3 John 1:2 (NKJV)
"Beloved, I pray that you may prosper in all things and be in health, just as your soul prospers."

You are body, soul, and spirit. Whenever you allow your soul to rule over your spirit and body, you are out of alignment. God's order is for the spirit to rule the soul and the soul to rule the body. Similar to the importance of spinal alignment, when you are out of spiritual alignment with God's Word emotional pain will be the result. Any violation of that order creates dysfunction. Dysfunction will eventually lead to pain.

Another purpose of pain is to prove that you are alive! Dead people have no feelings. Pain is a factual reality of life. You will not live without it. The Christian life is not about avoiding pain but rather how to endure until healing comes.

Pain can produce new life

When a woman is pregnant she has many changes occurring in her body. She is affected physically, mentally, and emotionally. For nine months she is going through discomfort. At the end of her pregnancy she will experience travail. Intense rhythmic pains bring forth new life. Her pain is turned into her greatest joy.

Whatever emotional pain you are experiencing now can give birth to something new in your life. The pain of your past will be used for your future purpose.

Paul refers to pain producing life in his relationship with the Galatians. Spiritually he was agonizing for them to have new life, to be like Jesus.

Galatians 4:19 (ESV)
"My little children, for whom I am again in the anguish of childbirth until Christ is formed in you!"

Could it be that the emotional pain that you are experiencing is because God is going to use you to minister to others?

2 Corinthians 1:4 (NLT)
"He comforts us in all our troubles so that we can comfort others. When they are troubled, we will be able to give them the same comfort God has given us."

Once you have given birth to new life, dreams, and hopes the pain of the past is forgotten because of the joy you are experiencing now.

John 16:21 (ESV)
"When a woman is giving birth, she has sorrow because her hour has come, but when she has delivered the baby,

she no longer remembers the anguish, for joy that a human being has been born into the world."

Using the pain of the past to bring new life will indeed lead to the pain free life.

PAIN IS A GUIDE THAT HELPS YOU LEARN FROM YOUR MISTAKES

"Without pain, there would be no suffering; without suffering we would never learn from our mistakes. To make it right, pain and suffering is the key to all windows, without it, there is no way of life." –**Angelina Jolie**

It can be a source that helps you to obtain excellence.

"My failure gave me strength; my pain was my motivation." –**Michael Jordan**

Samson by his loss of power, vision, and strength is taunted, humiliated, and mocked by his enemy. He who was once a deliverer is now a slave. A man who had the favor of God on his life and had the Holy Spirit come upon him mightily is found grinding at a mill in utter shame.

He had plenty of time to learn from his mistakes. When his hair began to grow again it reminded him of whom he used to be. He will not go down in defeat.

Judges 16:28 (NKJV)
"Then Samson called to the Lord, saying, 'O Lord God, remember me, I pray! Strengthen me, I pray, just this once, O God, that I may with one *blow* take vengeance on the Philistines for my two eyes!'"

God heard his emotional, pain-filled prayer and granted it. He killed more in his death than he had in his entire life. You may have made some serious mistakes that have embarrassed you and caused you great shame. The emotional pain may have lingered. Know that you are still alive. Your life continues to have purpose. God is not finished with you. Now you know how to do it right! Rise up from your ashes, servant of God, and get back in the game and get it right!

PAIN CREATES MOVEMENT

When you are in pain you cannot be still. You make every attempt to put yourself in a position that will bring relief. Emotional pain will either take you to a deeper relationship with the Lord or push you away from Him.

The Lord is not the source of your pain but He certainly will use it to draw you to himself. Paul was acquainted with the pain of suffering for the cause of Jesus. He was also acquainted with his own spiritual and emotional pain.

2 Corinthians 12:7 (ESV)
"So to keep me from becoming conceited because of the surpassing greatness of the revelations, a thorn was given me in the flesh, *a messenger of Satan* to *harass* me, to keep me from becoming conceited."

The King James Version chooses the word *buffet* in place of *harass*. The Greek word is *kolaphizol*. It means, "To strike with the fist, give one a blow with the fist; to maltreat, treat with violence and control."

I believe that Paul struggled with issues from his past. He had been responsible for persecuting believers with imprisonment and even death. You can never erase memories. Therefore, Satan would use his past memories to harass him.

Satan has no control over your present or future. **The only weapon Satan has to harass you is your past**. As a believer you are no longer under condem-nation (Romans 8:1). Your past life of sin has been forgiven. You are living life in the Spirit presently under grace. The Lord is ordering your steps for the future today.

How did Paul overcome the oppressive painful memories of his past? How did he silence the voice of his accuser?

2 Corinthians 12:8–9 (ESV)
"Three times I pleaded with the Lord about this, that it should leave me. ⁹ But he said to me, "My grace is sufficient for you, for my power is made perfect in weakness." Therefore I will boast all the more gladly of my weaknesses, so that the power of Christ may rest upon me.""

He overcame the past by the grace of God. Knowing that when he was at his weakest the power of Christ was resident in him. He was not suffering alone! He knew that suffering for Christ would bring a deeper relationship with Christ.

Philippians 3:10 (ESV)
"That I may know him and the power of his resurrection, and may share his sufferings, becoming like him in his death."

If the enemy knew that the secret to your success is pain he would not afflict you anymore.

Charles Spurgeon is without a doubt one of the greatest preachers of the gospel who ever lived. I am told that he preached more than six hundred times before he was twenty. He would regularly preach to six thousand in his Sunday service. It took sixty-three volumes to contain his sermons.

What was the secret to this man's success? Pain. His wife gives birth to twins and is unable to have any more children. When she was thirty-three years old she became an invalid. She was unable to attend church and seldom heard her husband preach. This condition would continue for twenty-seven years until she died.

Spurgeon himself suffered with gout, rheumatism, and Bright's disease. His greatest enemy was depression. He would weep by the hour and would not know why he wept. This continued until he died.

His explanation concerning his depression was that God used it, like He did with Paul, to keep him humble. It also was what God used to add power to his preaching. He concluded his opinion with the belief that it was a predictor of future blessing. He said that when he became depressed the Lord was about to add a larger blessing to his ministry.

You are not suffering in vain. God is going to bless others because of what you are discomforted with.

Pain is not an expression of God's punishment. It's the opportunity for an expression of His power.

Early in our marriage my wife and I lived in a duplex that my great uncle owned. He and his wife, Cliffie, lived in one apartment and my wife and I, in the other. Uncle Houston was a retired Nazarene preacher. His wife, Cliffie, suffered with rheumatoid arthritis since she was a young lady.

I recall many nights that I would be awakened by Aunt Cliffie crying out to God in her pain. She would praise Him. She would pray that others would not have her disease. This would happen often. I never met a more cheerful person or woman of faith than Aunt Cliffie. Never have I heard a woman pray with such power and anointing as she did.

PAIN CAN BECOME AN INSPIRATION FOR CREATIVITY

The pain of lost love has inspired many songs. Pain has inspired poetry and art. Hydraulics were invented to prevent muscle and back pain. New medications are continually being developed to relieve pain. Allow your pain to inspire avenues in your life that will ease the source of your pain.

PAIN CREATES CHANGE

There are two agents that will create change, desire and pain. My prayer for you is as you read this book you will be inspired by both. Pain, because you have reached a place that you refuse to accept a continuation of it. Desire, because the Lord is filling you with faith and hope that healing is indeed possible.

You have a decision to make. Are you going to ignore your emotional pain? Are you hoping it will go away in time or are you going admit you have it and seek God's help? Your decisions are deciding your stress. Your decisions affect your health.

Change is possible! The moment that you acknowledge you have emotional pain and look to the Word of God for healing you are on a path to a pain free life.

DISCUSSION QUESTIONS

1. Do you have physical or emotional pain?

2. What avenues have you taken to obtain healing?

3. How long have you experienced this pain?

4. How is the soul related to the health of the body?

5. What is the general cause of pain?

6. What are some positive benefits that come from pain?

7. What is determining your stress?

8. When does healing first begin?

CHAPTER 2

Discover The Source Of The Pain

———————

WHEN A CHILD IS INJURED one of the first questions that we ask is, "Where does it hurt?" We kiss it and encourage the child to believe that the pain is going to go away. However, the child may have a more serious injury than we first thought. It is possible to minimize the injury that needs attention. We may be putting a Band-Aid on a cancer.

There is a deceitfulness connected to how pain may manifest itself. Pain in a certain part of the body is not a clear indication that the cause of the pain is stemming from that specific area. How can that be? We have a central nervous system all throughout our body that can send false signals to other parts of the body.

A dentist told me that the pain I was experiencing on one side of my mouth was actually coming from the opposite side of my mouth. Pain that is running down the back of the leg may be caused by a sciatic nerve being pressed by vertebrae that is out of place in the middle of the back. Yet the back itself has no pain.

Before healing can occur, there must be a proper diagnosis. Have you ever self-diagnosed your pain? I think all of us have at some point in our life. During an examination the physician will ask, "What do you think is wrong with you? What meds have you taken for it?" Confident that we know what is wrong with us we are often surprised by the physician's diagnosis.

The medical field has a term "psychosomatic pain" that describes a person's pain that does not match his or her symptoms. This is often expressed by headaches, stomach and back pain. The treatment is usually antidepressants. Antidepressants shut down or suppress a person's emotions. It is basically minimizing their ability to feel.

Feelings can be deceiving because of the thoughts that create them. The following story indicates the power of our thoughts.

"Many years ago, a man was traveling across the country by sneaking from one freight train to the next. One night he climbed into what he thought was a boxcar. He closed the door, which automatically locked shut and trapped him inside. When his eyes adjusted to the light, he realized he was inside a refrigerated boxcar, and he became aware of the intense, freezing cold. He called for help and pounded on the door, but all the noise he made from the inside the car failed to attract anyone's attention. After many hours of struggle, he lay down on the floor of the railroad car.

As he tried to fight against the freezing cold, he scratched a message on the floor explaining his unfortunate, imminent death. Late the next day, repairmen from the railroad opened the door and found the dead man inside. Though the man had all the appearance of having frozen to death, the truth was the repairmen had come to fix the broken refrigerator unit in that car. Most likely the temperature of the railroad car had never fallen below fifty degrees during the night. The man had died because he *thought* he was freezing to death.

Perhaps nothing is more powerful in the world than the human mind. Your mind matters, and how you choose to think will have a major influence about nearly everything that happens in your life. The Bible says, "As he [a man] thinks in his heart, so is he" *(Proverbs 23:7, NKJV).*[1]

Too often we are treating the symptoms not the source of the affliction. It is either totally physical in nature or emotionally related.

---

1 "What Do You Have in Mind?," The Christian Broadcasting Network, accessed January 9, 2017, http://www1.cbn.com/family/what-do-you-have-in-mind%3F

Physical pain may be traced to a car accident, a fall, a blow to the head, etc.

Emotional pain will always be traced to an event that traumatized you.

All pain has its origin in original sin. Pain and death were introduced to Adam and Eve when they fell in the Garden of Eden. God told Eve, in Genesis 3:16 (ESV), "I will surely *multiply your pain* in childbearing; in pain you shall bring forth children." Adam is told in Genesis 3:17 (ESV), "Cursed is the ground because of you; *in pain* you shall eat of it all the days of your life."

Is there emotional pain when sin is committed? Observe the pain David shares with us and its effect on him.

Psalm 38:3–17 (NKJV)
"*3There is* no soundness in my flesh
Because of Your anger,
Nor *any* health in my bones
Because of my sin.
4For my iniquities have gone over my head;
Like a heavy burden they are too heavy for me.
5My wounds are foul *and* festering
Because of my foolishness.
6I am troubled, I am bowed down greatly;
I go mourning all the day long.

[7]For my loins are full of inflammation,
And *there is* no soundness in my flesh.
[8]I am feeble and severely broken;
I groan because of the turmoil of my heart.
[9]Lord, all my desire *is* before You;
And my sighing is not hidden from You.
[10]My heart pants, my strength fails me;
As for the light of my eyes, it also has gone from me.
[11]My loved ones and my friends stand aloof from my plague,
And my relatives stand afar off.
[12]Those also who seek my life lay snares *for me;*
Those who seek my hurt speak of destruction,
And plan deception all the day long.
[13]But I, like a deaf *man,* do not hear;
And *I am* like a mute *who* does not open his mouth.
[14]Thus I am like a man who does not hear,
And in whose mouth *is* no response.
[15]For in You, O Lord, I hope;
You will hear, O Lord my God.
[16]For I said, '*Hear me,* lest they rejoice over me,
Lest, when my foot slips, they exalt *themselves* against me.'
[17]For I *am* ready to fall,
And my sorrow *is* continually before me."

When Adam and Eve sinned they experienced loss of the garden, eternal life, the presence of God, and innocence. They became self-conscious. Gender rivalry began. The earth is cursed and so is man. Surely, they dealt with guilt and remorse because of their disobedience.

Emotional distress, also called "mental anguish," describes very real injuries suffered by victims due to the negligent or willful acts of another.

Adam and the earth suffer for Eve's decision to disobey God. Adam and Eve experience grief and death after Cain murders his brother Abel. Again, they are reminded of how one's wrong doing can damage the emotions of others.

Are you suffering from the acts of others, such as, sexual violation, physical abuse, abandonment, anger, forced isolation, hunger, poverty, divorce, or continually being lied to?

The following are some of the symptoms of emotional distress.

* Anxiety
* Depression
* Guilt
* Fear
* Insomnia
* Bitterness
* Jealousy
* Rage

Do you claim ownership to any of these? Do you mask your pain? By that I mean, are you denying to others that you have pain? Do you deny that anything happened at all? These are feeble attempts to suppress and conceal pain.

I was the pastor of a young man who was bullied at school. His outward appearance and personality would never reflect what he was feeling on the inside. This is a poem he wrote expressing his true feelings.

IF THEY ONLY KNEW

As I sit here all alone
I wonder what went wrong
I've got the clothes,
I've got the shoes,
I've got everything popular kids do.

Some call me stupid
Some call me ignorant
How am I to take this?
If only they knew the real me,
I'm fun and cheerful
But they only look at the outward appearance.

They say I'm fat,
I'm ugly,
And have a big butt.

If only they knew that I'm trying to change.
My grades aren't the best in the world,
But does that really matter?
I think not.

Should these kids bother me?
Everyone says, "No".
But they do—Oh, how they do!
If they only know how much they do.

I've had all this I can take,
I've just about reached the end.
I'm up against the wall.
Cliché, cliché,
My soul speaks only in cliché.

Goodbye.
My duty calls.
I have to go take some more.
If they only knew—
Oh, if they only knew.

Bryan Hill

Why do we put cosmetics on corpses for funerals? It is our attempt to make them look as alive as possible. The reality is that we are only concealing decay. We do not want to deal with the reality of what death actually looks like.

Men are especially private with their pain. They do not share their hurts as women do. It is not 'manly' to admit pain and weakness. Men say:

* "I'll make it!"
* "I will just have to suck it up and move on."
* "I will deal with it my own way."
* "I don't need anyone's help."

It is not uncommon for people to mask their pain with laughter. Most well-known comedians have experienced great emotional pain in their past and their way of masking it is comedy or humor.

*"My parents' divorce left me with a lot of sadness and pain and acting, and especially humor, was my way of dealing with all that." – **Jennifer Aniston***

I remember as a child that I couldn't wait till Sunday afternoon when all my father's siblings and their children would gather at my grandfather's home for lunch. The house would be filled with stories of their childhood. They all had a funny story and used laughter to hide the reality of pain hidden in their hearts. It wasn't until I became an adult that I learned of the painful experiences that they all shared. They were a large farming family living in poverty because of a father who was a physically and verbally abusive alcoholic.

Their way of masking the pain was laughter. With what are you masking your pain? Alcohol? Drugs? Sex? Food? Money? Could these methods be called "pain killers"? They make you feel good. They are an escape from having to live in the real world. The danger of using these methods for pain suppression is that they may become addictive.

You must go deeper than the manifestation of pain. Deep inside you is pain that had a starting place. When did you begin to experience the emotional pain? What was happening in your life at that time? Were you a victim of a circumstance that you could not control? Are you living with guilt for the trauma you brought into someone else's life?

Don't be surprised if some of the root cause for the emotional stress leads to your own door.

*"One of the ways that people avoid taking responsibility for their role in their own pain is what I call the –BPs— blame and projection." –***Iyanla Vanzant**

Our natural tendency is to blame others when we are really attempting to avoid responsibility for our own decision or actions that caused the pain. We say such things as, "If they hadn't made me angry I wouldn't have...", "If you hadn't said that to me I wouldn't have...".

Wasn't this Adam's response to the loss of the garden? He blamed God because He created the woman who fell.

Genesis 3:12 (NKJV)
"Then the man said, 'The woman whom You gave *to be* with me, she gave me of the tree, and I ate.'"

You must take responsibility for your actions that have caused others emotional pain.

What is the source of *your* pain? Is it physically induced? Is your emotional pain coming from being a victim of a trauma? Is the source of your emotional pain rooted in personal failure, sin, or making a victim of others?

Pain does not come to remain. It is temporary. If it is related to sin, repent and don't continue to repeat the action. If medical tests fail to reveal a cause for the pain, it may have originated because of emotional trauma. In this case, immediately seek help from a qualified source.

How quickly the pain is removed depends upon how quickly you choose to take action against it.

Regardless of the source, pain is still pain. Once you have determined the source of the pain you can progress toward a cure. Your peace is more important than driving yourself crazy trying to figure out why something happened the way it did. Let it go!

In the ensuing chapters, we will deal with how to live the pain free life.

DISCUSSION QUESTIONS

1. What is the deceitfulness of pain?

2. What is psychosomatic pain?

3. What is emotional pain always connected with?

4. What are some symptoms of emotional stress?

5. What are some ways that people mask their pain?

6. What are the two sources of pain?

7. What emotional pain are you dealing with?

8. Are you going to seek help and healing for it?

CHAPTER 3

Remove The Pain Of Anger

———◆———

"You can't see your reflection in boiling water. Similarly, you can't see the truths in your life in a state of anger." **–Bishop Dale Bonner**

SAUL OF TARSUS WAS AN angry man. He was so blinded by religious pride that he could not see his own spiritual condition. He was so full of anger toward Christians that threatened the Jewish faith. He consented to the stoning of Stephen. Paul describes his passion against Christians in Acts 22:4 (KJV), "And I persecuted this way unto the death, binding and delivering into prisons both men and women."

On the road to Damascus, Saul had a personal encounter with Jesus. He heard a voice and saw a bright light. As a result, he was humbled with blindness for three days. Ananias is sent to where Saul is lodging and he prays for him. Scripture says that *scales* fell off of Saul's eyes and he could see.

This is just conjecture on my part, but I believe that the scales that fell off of his eyes were a physical manifestation of what was taking place in his spiritual life. He was blinded because of his knowledge.

Saul had been "a Pharisee of Pharisees". He states in Philippians 3:5-6 (KJV), "Circumcised the eighth day, of the stock of Israel, of the tribe of Benjamin, an Hebrew of the Hebrews; as touching the law, a Pharisee; concerning zeal, persecuting the church; touching the righteousness which is in the law, blameless."

Saul had been blinded. After the scales of pride are removed he can take on a new identity in Christ, know the will of God, and pursue his life assignment spoken over him by Ananias.

Jesus told us in reference to judging a brother to remove the log out of our own eye before we attempt to take a splinter out of our brother's eye. Before healing can take place, whatever is embedded in us emotionally must be removed. Many people would already be healed of their emotional pain if they had only taken the initiative to remove the object at the onset rather than allowing it to become a part of them.

There are those who attend healing conferences with the expectation the minister is going to lay hands on them and instantly they will be healed of their emotional pain. Before God can do His part in the healing process we must do ours first. The promise has already been given that healing will take place when we remove the issue that is lodged in our soul.

Ecclesiastes 11:10 (ESV)
"Remove vexation from your heart, and put away pain from your body."

In this passage of Scripture Solomon is addressing the issue of vexation. Vexation in Hebrew is *ka'as* meaning "grief, anger, sorrow, provoking, and spite".

The anger that I am addressing is not from a malfunction of the body such as a brain tumor or other stimuli. I am addressing anger totally from a spiritual perspective.

I recently was flown to a major city to do an emotional healing for a man that the pastor said was the angriest man he had ever met. I was ambivalent about meeting the man, so I took a team member with me. During the session, the pastor would walk past the room we were using to make sure we were safe.

The candidate was at first disrespectful and hateful. Not knowing what was about to happen, he was filled with questions. He attempted to take control of the session.

He had been a well-known evangelist in his denomination. He had left the ministry and was now self-employed.

Like Jonah, this man was not walking in his destiny or calling. He was the right man in the wrong place. Living out of the will of God is painful. He had been in the storm. His life was filled with heartache and disappointment. Having experienced divorce and rejection by his denomination and minister friends, he embarked on a path of bad decisions that had added even more to his emotional pain.

I also discovered that from his childhood he had struggled with his identity because of the rejection of his father. Though at the time he was a middle-aged man, he remained angry because of his father's continued rejection.

To help this man be set free and healed of his anger required that we teach him the source of his anger.

"Why am I so angry?", is a good question to ask yourself. The source of your anger may not be what you think. Anger, like a plant, has many roots. What are the roots anger stems from? Some are visible and others are unseen or beneath the surface.

First, anger is a generational sin. Does anger run through your family tree as much as three generations? It is a learned behavior. Therefore, anger must be dealt with because it will affect your future posterity. This is not what you want to pass on to the next generation. By example, previous generations have taught, "This is how you express your anger." It must stop with you.

Fear may also be a root that triggers anger. When a child is bullied, he will react in one of two ways. He will withdraw within himself or he will boil over with anger and retaliate. Knowing that he's going to be bullied regardless of what he does he chooses to become angry. He begins to fight back without concern of payback. He has taken all he can take. Fear will use anger as a defensive mechanism.

I was dealing with a man in an emotional healing session who had tattoos all over his body. He was a very large man, tall and muscular. Because of his appearance, he had an intimidating presence.

I asked him why he had so many tattoos. His response surprised me. He said, "I come from a very large family. I never received much attention from my parents. I was bullied all through school and never felt accepted. Throughout my teenage years, because I was timid and withdrawn, the bullying continued. During this time, I began to grow taller and develop muscles by lifting weights. I added all of these tattoos because I think when people see a big man with tattoos they fear them. I don't want people bullying me."

Though he did not appear to be angry there was deep anger embedded inside of him that needed to be released. He had responded the only way he knew how to protect himself. As the session continued the Lord ministered to him in a very powerful way and set him free from his anger.

If anger is not conquered it will escalate.

Colossians 3:8 (KJV)
"But now ye also put off all these; anger, wrath, malice."

Notice in this passage the degrees of anger.

1. Anger is a feeling that is oriented toward some real or supposed grievance.
2. Wrath is when anger is elevated to rage. It is anger intensified.
3. Malice is the intent to do harm.

Do not permit anger to build up over a lengthy period of time. Deal with it quickly.

Jealousy is a root of anger. Solomon informs us that **jealousy is a fear of being replaced by someone else.**

Proverbs 6:34 (NKJV)
"For jealousy is a husband's fury; Therefore he will not spare in the day of vengeance."

Anger that comes from the passion of love being infringed upon, desires to destroy anything or anyone that threatens it.

Song of Solomon 8:6 (NKJV)
"Jealousy is as cruel as the grave."

Do you have fear of being replaced in a relationship? If you have been betrayed in a relationship most likely there is a very hostile anger lodged in your spirit.

Another root of anger is pride. The person who is prideful is a controller. If the controller does not have control he will take control with displays of anger. Whatever it takes for his will to be established he will use it. Whether it is physical force, verbal threatening, tantrums, etc. Anger is used to gain control.

People attempt to justify their displays of anger with a weak apology, however, anger is like a shotgun blast. It only lasts for a second but it destroys everything in front of it. You may apologize for the acts of anger but the devastation lingers.

If the manifestation of anger is rooted in pride the person who is angry will always justify their actions. The reason is because pride is all about me. It will come forth in these words, "They deserved it."

Do you have issues with control?

The subtlety of anger is that it is not always displayed outwardly. It may be internalized. This is depression. Webster's dictionary defines depression as suppressed anger. On the surface one appears to be calm and timid. On the inside a storm is raging.

Grief is also a root of anger. Grief is related to loss. Examples of loss would be: the loss of a family member, a job, sexual innocence, or even loss of health to mention a few. What these losses have in common is something has been taken from you without your permission.

When anger is suppressed it turns into bitterness. You know what the bitterness is!

Proverbs 14:10 (ESV)
"The heart knows its own bitterness."

Your bitterness will affect many others.

Hebrews 12:15 (ESV)
"See to it that no one fails to obtain the grace of God; that no "root of bitterness" springs up and causes trouble, and by it many become defiled."

Bitterness is aggressive. It "springs up." It causes trouble. Remember that the life of the believer is blessed with the fruit of the Spirit. The first mentioned is love, joy and peace. This fruit of the spirit is choked when the root of bitterness is allowed to remain. The heart becomes hard, unfeeling, and carnal in nature. Get rid of bitterness!

The anger from your grief and bitterness is therefore focused on the individual who is responsible for your loss. Whom are you angry with? Are you angry with yourself, someone else, or God? What has been taken from you without your permission? The answer to these questions will help you to understand why you are angry.

Now that you have a better understanding concerning anger it is time to confront and eradicate it.

Ecclesiastes11:10 (ESV)
"Remove vexation from your heart"

How can you remove vexation? First begin by taking responsibility for it. You have yielded your body to house anger and exhibit it. It is your body that has become the container of this toxic emotion. It was your tongue, your fist, and your facial expression that you used to express your anger.

Romans 6:13 (NLT)
"Do not let any part of your body become an instrument of evil to serve sin. Instead, give yourselves completely to God, for you were dead, but now you have new life. So use your whole body as an instrument to do what is right for the glory of God."

Your body belongs to the Lord by redemption. You have been bought with a price, the precious blood of Jesus. Yet, you are responsible for what you do with it. It is not the devil's; it is yours! The body responds according to your will. No one forced your body to serve sin. You yielded it to sin. You must be the one who removes it. You are the one who allowed it to enter your heart!

You can remove anger from your heart by allowing grace to teach you.

Titus 2:11–12 (ESV)
"For the grace of God has appeared, bringing salvation for all people, training us to renounce ungodliness and worldly passions, and to live self-controlled, upright, and godly lives in the present age,"

Grace teaches you that you can deny yourself! It teaches you to say "No!" to being out of control. Allow the grace of God to teach you self-control.

Anger will be removed from your heart when you think before you act or respond. Anger is impulsive behavior. You *can* rule your own spirit.

Proverbs 16:32 (KJV)
"He that is slow to anger is better than the mighty; And he that ruleth his spirit than he that taketh a city."

How do you learn to rule or control your anger? By submitting to the discipline of the Father.

Proverbs 3:11 (ESV)
"My son, do not despise the Lᴏʀᴅ's discipline or be weary of his reproof,"

Hebrews 12:5–6 (ESV)
"And have you forgotten the exhortation that addresses you as sons? 'My son, do not regard lightly the discipline of the Lord, nor be weary when reproved by him. For the Lord disciplines the one he loves, and chastises every son whom he receives.'"

The Lord does not discipline without giving instruction. My father had a saying that contains this truth. He said, "Those who cannot hear can feel." Those who will not listen to reproof will suffer the consequences.

Pain makes the wise listen. Listening will allow you to avoid pain. The tuition in the school of experience is too costly. Learn at others' expense.

Jeremiah 30:12,15,17 (NKJV)
"12 For thus says the Lᴏʀᴅ:
'Your affliction is incurable,
Your wound is severe.
15 Why do you cry about your affliction?

Your sorrow is incurable.
Because of the multitude of your iniquities,
Because your sins have increased,
I have done these things to you.
¹⁷ For I will restore health to you
And heal you of your wounds,' says the LORD."

The pain of discipline will change behavior and actions. When anger is allowed a free hand in your life you will suffer the consequences of your actions. Because God loves you and wants to spare you of future pain He will bring discipline and instruction to your life. Receive it and submit to it.

Anger is a habit. They say it takes twenty-one days to break a habit. A habit is broken when we change the way we think. As a man thinks in his heart so is he. You must take control of your mind.

2 Corinthians 10:5 (ESV)
"We destroy arguments and every lofty opinion raised against the knowledge of God, and take every thought captive to obey Christ."

Your behavior is established by how the body responds to a thought. Cast down the thought that defies God's Word. Right behavior comes from a mind that is slow to anger.

Proverbs 19:11 (ESV)
"Good sense makes one slow to anger, and it is his glory to overlook an offense."

Channel your energy to do good and not evil. Anger is permitted.

Ephesians 4:26 (ESV)
"Be angry and do not sin; do not let the sun go down on your anger."

Your anger is permitted but not to a point of sinning with it. It has a time limit on it. Don't end the day with anger in your heart. Anger is a choice. It can be restrained. God himself exercises anger but in righteousness. The following verse teaches us a great deal.

Isaiah 48:9 (ESV)
"For my name's sake I defer my anger; for the sake of my praise I restrain it for you, that I may not cut you off."

God says He will set aside His anger in honor of His own name. Does your name and reputation mean anything to you? Anger out of control will cost you your reputation. He goes on to say that He defers anger for the purpose of keeping Israel in relationship with Him. Do you want to keep your relationship with God healthy? Guard your anger for His name's sake.

Use the focus of your anger for righteous causes. For example, Mothers Against Drunk Driving (MADD), Amber Alert, Lonesome Dove Ranch, and many other similar organizations have been established out of personal pain. They focused the energy of their anger on helping instead of destroying.

When the anger has been removed, peace is restored. Your body will not be continually tense. Your blood pressure will drop. You will begin to feel good about yourself because you are not permitting others to affect your emotions.

Remove the destructive anger and allow your righteous anger to work for you.

Discussion Questions

1. What is the definition for vexation?

2. What are the three levels of anger?

3. What is generational anger?

4. What are the roots of anger?

5. What are the two roots of anger that are suppressed?

6. What is the first step to removing anger?

7. How do I remove anger out of my heart?

8. What good can come out of anger?

CHAPTER 4

Release To Be At Peace

———

YOUR LIFE IN CHRIST IS like a balloon without air. You can stomp on it and it retains its shape. It continues to have the capacity to hold air. You can pull and stretch it, and it will hold its shape. The believer is flexible in life. He continues to be resilient and maintain his composure. The believer is at his best when the pressure is not on the inside of him.

A balloon is made to contain limited pressure. As long as the pressure is within its limits the balloon will float into the air. God will use the pressures of life to elevate you. However, when the pressure inside the balloon exceeds its limits it will burst.

The same is true when the pressure inside of you becomes more than you can bear; you will shatter emotionally. If you don't learn to release, it will increase the level of emotional stress and pain. If you choose to hold on to the pain and refuse to release it to God, nothing changes.

*"What you let go of tends to not get repeated.... hold on to bad stuff and you will see it again." –***Dr. Henry Cloud**

You will be at your best when you learn to release the stress and pressure that is built up within you.

RELEASE BY CASTING

1 Peter 5:7 (ESV)
"Casting all your anxieties on him, because he cares for you."

The Lord will help you when you cast *all* your anxieties on Him. The word cast is a word that implies force or power. You have the authority through Christ to cast your cares upon Him. Again, the Lord does not want *some* of your anxieties; He wants *all* of them.

The goal of the surgeon when he is removing cancer is to get it all. If a root of cancer remains it will continue to spread throughout the body and end in death.

Another analogy would be the storm that Paul and the Roman soldiers encountered on their way to Rome. The storm came suddenly upon them and for days they did not see the sun, moon or stars. They were in peril of losing their lives. How would they survive?

Acts 27:18–20 (ESV)
"Since we were violently storm-tossed, they began the next day to jettison the cargo. And on the third day they threw the ship's tackle overboard with their own hands. When neither sun nor stars appeared for many days, and no small tempest lay on us, all hope of our being saved was at last abandoned."

They first cast overboard some of the cargo. As the storm continued they were forced to take stronger measures. Then the tackle for operating the ship was cast overboard. Fourteen days later, Paul has an angelic visitation and is told that all who stay on the ship will live. They let down four anchors hoping to slow the ship down before hitting land. Some of the sailors made their way into lifeboats hoping to make it to land. Paul commands the centurion to cut the ropes holding the lifeboats and let them go. He then tells them to eat, then throw the wheat overboard. The last saving step was to cut the ropes that held four anchors and raise the sails to hit the reef. True to the angel's words, all who remained on the ship lived.

Consider what they released, and the order in which they did so. First, they gave the cargo to the sea. The cargo would be unnecessary weight. Jesus instructs us in Hebrews 12:1 (ESV), "Let us also lay aside every weight, and sin which clings so closely."

Don't hold on to the memories, the people, sin, and events that have brought you pain. Give them to the sea! It will cover all you place in it. Are these memories and events mountains in your life that do not move? If you have faith in Christ's finished work on the cross they will be moved. He came to destroy the works of the enemy. Have faith in what He has already done for you.

Matthew 21:21 (ESV)
"And Jesus answered them, 'Truly, I say to you, if you have faith and do not doubt, you will not only do what has been done to the fig tree, but even if you say to this mountain, 'Be taken up and thrown into the sea,' it will happen.'"

Do you see the picture? How tall is your mountain? Observe what happens to it when you use the name of Jesus. It will be plucked up and thrown into the sea. As tall as that mountain is you cannot see it! Why? The sea covers it.

The next step they took was to cast the tackle into the sea. The tackle is what they used to operate the ship. To become pain free release all of your human effort in attempting to save yourself. You, like Paul, have a destiny. Instead of struggling in your own effort to save yourself trust the Master of the sea. He will do for you what you cannot do for yourself.

This storm would linger. Your pain has lingered for a lengthy season. Fourteen days into the storm Paul receives a word from God. When you trust God in your storm you will receive a word from Him. It will be the word that delivers you.

Four anchors are then let down to slow the speed of the ship. This would be a temporary rest for them. Some soldiers were getting in lifeboats to attempt to save themselves. Paul tells the captain if they don't stay with the ship they will die. The captain has the ropes of the lifeboats cut. Again, they had to let go, or release what they thought would save their lives.

How many attempts have you made trying to get out of your storm? While the anchors provide them with rest, they are told to eat. Paul takes bread, blesses it and they all eat. They not only needed rest, but to be fed. Why? They had not eaten since they had been in the storm. The storm had completely exhausted them until they no longer had hope of survival. Acts 27:36 states, "They were all of good cheer." In other words their strength was renewed and their spirits were lifted. Your strength is in the Word of God. When you are struggling to release everything to God your faith must be established in His Word.

Now, they are at their most critical moment of survival. They continue to cast overboard and release the unnecessary weight, including all their food supply, into the sea (v. 38). There is nothing left! Now it is win or lose. It is live or die.

Acts 27:40 (NKJV)
"And they let go the anchors and left them in the sea, meanwhile loosing the rudder ropes; and they hoisted the mainsail to the wind and made for shore."

You see that? They had already committed all they had to the sea, now they are giving *themselves*. The result? They all would be saved on pieces of the ship or by swimming to shore. None were lost just as the angel told Paul.

I have a word for you. When you give it all to Jesus you too are going make it.

RELEASE THE OFFENDER

To become pain free, you must release not just the offense but the offender as well. I was visiting a man in the hospital and the conversation turned toward a man that God and the church had forgiven. As we talked I discerned he was challenging God for forgiving this man of his offense. I spoke plainly to him, "Your problem is not with God forgiving him. Your problem is that you don't want to forgive him." Surprisingly he admitted to it.

The pain free life is continuing to forgive before forgiveness is needed. Forgiveness is not a one-time event. It is an ongoing process. You will struggle with forgiveness when you are forgiving a repeat offender. To forgive knowing they will repeat the offense and seek forgiveness again is trying to say the least.

Jesus addressed repeat offenders and forgiveness.

Matthew 18:21–22 (ESV)
"Then Peter came up and said to him, 'Lord, how often will my brother sin against me, and I forgive him? As many as seven times?' Jesus said to him, 'I do not say to you seven times, but seventy-seven times.'"

We are to forgive as often as we would desire to be forgiven. Jesus stated it in the Lord's Prayer.

Matthew 6:14–15 (ESV)
"For if you forgive others their trespasses, your heavenly Father will also forgive you, but if you do not forgive others their trespasses, neither will your Father forgive your trespasses."

How many times have you come before the Lord and asked forgiveness? It will probably not be the last time.

It is difficult to forgive people who refuse to admit that they are wrong. A little girl got into trouble with her mother for not obeying. Her mother put her in the clothes closet to teach her a lesson. Soon Dad opened the closet door and asked her, "What are you doing in here?" To which she responded, "I have been spitting on all of mother's clothes and was standing here waiting on more spit!" It is a crude story but clearly represents the attitude of a person who refuses to accept responsibility for their wrong.

Don't expect them to say, "I am sorry" or "Please forgive me." You must forgive because you too will need forgiveness.

It is difficult to forgive those who have willfully and intentionally hurt you. They show no remorse. Of course, we will never be more like Jesus and Stephen than when we pray, "Father forgive them because they do not know what they are doing".

To forgive is love; not to forgive is judging.

You must be reminded the judgment you render to others will be reciprocated to you (Matthew 7:2). When you give forgiveness, you forgo the right of judging. This allows God to become the judge. His promise is justice.

Romans 12:19 (ESV)
"Beloved, never avenge yourselves, but leave it to the wrath of God, for it is written, 'Vengeance is mine, I will repay, says the Lord.'"

Because you have forgiven doesn't mean you have to rebuild a relationship with them. You will not be disappointed when you follow a scriptural pattern for dealing with your offender.

The closer the relationship is to the offender the more intense the pain. A pastor hired a close friend to work with him on his church staff. Later, the pastor, in the best interest of the church and the staff member, fired him. His friend would not have much to do with him and the staff member's wife would not speak to him. After giving them a farewell, and attempting to keep the friendship, they lingered by a stage curtain to visit. The wife of the staff member became irate, and began to kick the pastor and scream at him for firing them.

The pastor was so disturbed by the incident that he sought counsel to help him process the matter. After hearing the story the counselor said, "They must have loved you very much." In shock the pastor asked, "How can you say that?" He replied, "The anger that was expressed was because they placed such value on your friendship. Their pain was stimulated by the false perception that you didn't love them."

Release Yourself From Guilt

A victim will assume the guilt for what the offender has done. For instance, a child who is abused will assume guilt that he must have done something wrong therefore deserving what was done to him. A wife who is continually verbally abused by her husband eventually begins to believe there must be something wrong with her.

Guilt is placed on the victim by the offender's words. Words like, "I wouldn't have done it if you hadn't said that." "You made me do it!" "It is all your fault!" "If you weren't so stupid this wouldn't have happened!"

That is false guilt! You don't have to bear that anymore. Stop blaming yourself for what you are not guilty of! You are not responsible for your parents' divorce. You are not responsible for your parents' poverty or financial loss. You are not responsible for your siblings because you left home. You are not responsible because an adult violated you as a child.

Stop feeling guilty for the sexual abuse of your spouse to you or others. There is nothing wrong with you! You did not deserve it!

What if you *were* guilty? Take heart. We all have been guilty of wrongdoing. There is a remedy. The remedy is having faith in the blood of Jesus to cleanse us of our sin. We may live with the consequences of our actions but we do not have to carry the guilt the rest of our lives.

Repentance removes guilt. Before God we stand blameless in Christ. Remember the devil has only the past to use as a weapon against you. He is the accuser of the brethren. You have an advocate, the man, Christ Jesus, who intercedes to the Father on your behalf. He bore your sins and your judgment on the cross.

To repent means to have a change of mind or to convert. You no longer continue to repeat willful sin. You have been forgiven. Because of the Father's forgiveness you can forgive yourself. You are not the same person of your past. Claim your worthiness to be at the table of the Lord.

1 Corinthians 6:9–11 (ESV)
"Or do you not know that the unrighteous will not inherit the kingdom of God? Do not be deceived: neither the sexually immoral, nor idolaters, nor adulterers, nor men who practice homosexuality, nor thieves, nor the greedy, nor drunkards, nor revilers, nor swindlers will inherit the kingdom of God. And such were some of you. But you were washed, you were sanctified, you were justified in the name of the Lord Jesus Christ and by the Spirit of our God."

As long as you assume the guilt, whether it is false guilt or true guilt, you will not live the pain free life. Turn it loose in Jesus' name.

RELEASE THE EMOTION CONNECTED TO THE OFFENSE FROM THE BODY

Not knowing how to deal with their inner pain people turn to cutting, anorexia, bulimia, or compulsive behavior. These methods to release pain fail because the pain is merely transferred elsewhere. It remains.

The main factor to releasing offense is doing whatever it takes to get it out of the body. I suggest that you try the following methods of releasing whatever the emotion is.

One method you may want to use is to get alone, and take an object that is cheap and tear it to pieces. Don't stop until you are at peace.

A second method is to take a pillow and beat the floor with it once for each year of your life. While doing so speak to the person who hurt you and tell them the feelings that you have dealt with all these years.

A lady came to us for help dealing with depression. She had a great deal of suppressed anger. Her family had been under public scrutiny. She was a pastor's wife who had hurt so deeply for so long. She had been made fun of, told she wasn't good enough nor pretty enough. She was not musical and did not live up to people's expectations of what they thought a pastor's wife was supposed to be and do. She had suffered personal loss and dealt with it privately. She felt as though she was living in a glass house.

When we encouraged her to use the pillow, as I previously stated she spoke to each offender. She told them what they said and how badly she was wounded by their words and judgment of her. She released that pent-up anger through the use of that pillow hitting the floor. She was being given a voice that had been silenced. She was putting her pain into words to those who had hurt her. She used the pillow so much her knuckles bled.

After releasing her anger using this method she was weeping and exhausted. I asked her, "How do you feel?" She said, "I feel so relaxed. I feel like the world has been lifted off of me. I feel so good."

A third method is to get where no one can see or hear you and scream as long and as loud as you can, three times. Why? It is a form of relieving inner stress. It is letting the pressure out of the balloon.

The balloon, that we opened this chapter with, may be a fourth method of releasing inward pain to our Father. Get alone where no one will see or hear you. Name the pain and blow it into the balloon. Rejection, sexual abuse, divorce, depression, verbal abuse, abandonment, being controlled, grief, anger, fear, etc., are just a few.

When you have filled the balloon pinch it so the air does not escape and hold. Hold it up in the air and begin to claim the healing power of Jesus. Declare that this is no longer a part of your life and you are releasing it to God. Release the balloon. It becomes a visual of what God does with your sins and your pain. It suddenly begins to move away from you. It goes upward. It will fall empty to the ground.

By confessing faith in the completed work of Calvary your life is like that balloon. The pressure is no longer in it. It has kept its shape and it is relaxed.

This is only a simple method but the symbolism will be an act of faith that sets you free. Release and be at peace!

DISCUSSION QUESTIONS

1. What does it mean to "cast your cares on the Lord"?

2. What are the sequences of which Paul conditioned the ship to save lives?

3. How do I release my offender?

4. Who are the three most difficult types of people to forgive?

5. How do you overcome false guilt?

6. How does one forgive themselves of their own guilt?

7. How do I release the emotional pain from my body?

CHAPTER 5

Retreat To Not Repeat

"Our emotional response is driven by the proximity of events." —**Piyush Shrivastav**

TO RETREAT IS TO SEPARATE, to withdraw or to distance from. Distancing yourself from the offender may be necessary for your healing.

It is one thing to deal with the pain of a memory and another to be present with the one who created the memory. Jacob deceives his brother Esau out of his birthright for the price of a bowl of beans. To make matters worse a short time later he deceives Isaac and steals Esau's patriarchal blessing.

When Esau discovers what Jacob has done he desires to kill him. From the womb Jacob has been grabbing the heel of Esau. Now that he has Esau's birthright and blessing Jacob flees for his life to his mother's people.

Genesis 27:41 (ESV)
"Now Esau hated Jacob because of the blessing with which his father had blessed him, and Esau said to himself, 'The days of mourning for my father are approaching; then I will kill my brother Jacob.'"

Jacob works for Laban to obtain two wives, Leah and Rachel. He prospers to such a degree that he leaves Laban to establish his own home. They have been separated twenty years from Esau. Jacob now sends word to Esau by his messengers to appease his anger.

Genesis 32:4 (ESV)
"Instructing them, Thus you shall say to my lord Esau: Thus says your servant Jacob, 'I have sojourned with Laban and stayed until now.'"

Note he speaks with humility, "your servant Jacob." When the servants return, they tell Jacob that Esau is coming to meet him with four hundred men. Jacob was afraid and greatly distressed. He divides his wealth and his family into three divisions so that all will not be lost.

With what he had left he would attempt to appease Esau's wrath. He would send an elaborate gift. Three or four groups of animals would be given to him. If he asked where Jacob was the response was to be, "Your servant is behind us."

Jacob is scheduled to meet his brother the next morning. In the night Jacob's life would be changed forever. He would wrestle with an angel all night till the dawning. He would receive a new identity. He would no longer be Jacob, meaning deceiver, but Israel, prince of God. He also would be marked by the experience. The remainder of his life he would walk with a limp because the angel had touched his thigh.

If the two men had remained in proximity to one another, one of them would have been killed. By the providence of God, Jacob would receive his father's blessing and keep his life. Time and distance would allow the pain of deceit to be dealt with. Because of time and distance both men had changed. God has dramatically changed Jacob, and Esau could detect it.

It is thrilling to watch the two reunited. It did not play out like Jacob had expected. When you have had a life-changing encounter with God everything in your life changes.

Remember they are twins. The bond that twins share is so unique and special. Watch what happens when they meet?

Genesis 33:3–4 (ESV)
"He himself went on before them, bowing himself to the ground seven times, until he came near to his brother. But

Esau ran to meet him and embraced him and fell on his neck and kissed him, and they wept."

Jacob approaches Esau in fear and humility but Esau runs to him. They hug, kiss and cry! Only God can do that. What a picture of reconciliation.

This would never have happened had it not been for Jacob's encounter with God that changed his identity. He was a different person indeed. Remember that Jacob has encountered God but Esau has not. He was the same man.

Observe the wisdom Jacob used in this moment when damaged emotions are being healed and reconciliation is taking place.

Genesis 33:14–17 (ESV)
"'Let my lord pass on ahead of his servant, and I will lead on slowly, at the pace of the livestock that are ahead of me and at the pace of the children, until I come to my lord in Seir.' So Esau said, 'Let me leave with you some of the people who are with me.' But he said, 'What need is there? Let me find favor in the sight of my lord.' So Esau returned that day on his way to Seir. But Jacob journeyed to Succoth, and built himself a house and made booths for his livestock. Therefore the name of the place is called Succoth."

Esau wanted Jacob to live with him in Seir. Jacob attempts to waffle out of it by telling him to go on ahead and he will follow at a slower pace. Esau continues to reach out to Jacob and offered to leave some of his people to help him. Jacob knew that they could not dwell peaceably together. Having made peace and reconciliation with Esau, Jacob settles in a different place than his brother.

The pain free life is in knowing some you have reconciled with are not to be close to you. When you know that the one who caused you pain has not changed, distance yourself from that person and be at peace. Don't lose your wholeness attempting to change a person who does not want to be changed.

Reconciliation is not always possible. When you have forgiven and addressed the offender in love their response is their responsibility, not yours. Their reaction may not be favorable. Distance yourself from them and move on with your life.

David is brought into the family of King Saul after he defeats Goliath. He did not know that the next few years of his life a man he honored and loved would be a continual threat to his life. Saul out of jealous rage attempts no less than five times to kill David.

On two occasions David had Saul's life in his hands. He could have killed him but did not because he was God's anointed king. David would attempt to reason with him but it was in vain. Even Saul himself admitted that David was not worthy of the way he was treating him. In front of the entire army he told David that he was an honorable man. Yet nothing changed.

For David to keep his life and peace of mind he must distance himself from Saul as much as possible. Saul would not change.

You may have a circumstance of spousal abuse. You have been on the receiving end of vented anger, physical or sexual abuse. Your spouse repeatedly apologizes and asks for forgiveness. Promises are made that it will not happen again. Yet it does. What is to be done? Distance yourself from the problem, separate. The purpose for separation is for reconciliation.

You must retreat or distance yourself for relief. When you remain near the offender your mind will constantly be questioning your role in the issue. The devil will cloud your mind and create self-doubt. The longer the time and distance you are away from the offender and the place of offense the greater the rest. Physically and mentally you will be at peace. Separation from the offender does not heal the wound but does allow you the advantage of processing how to deal with it. This also allows God to work on the offender. Your responsibility is not to correct the offender but to take the necessary steps for your own healing.

The pain free life does not allow the offender in a place for the offense to be repeated.

* You do not allow the thief, that stole from you, to handle your money again.
* You do not allow the adulterer to be alone with your spouse.
* You do not allow the pedophile, that molested you, near your children.
* You do not allow a gossip, who betrayed your confidence, access to privileged information.
* You do not allow the alcoholic, who beat you, to be near alcoholic beverages.

Do not allow your emotional connection with the offender to override your good judgment. **You stop attracting certain people when you heal the parts of you that once needed them.**

You will have a pain free life when you no longer have an emotional need for the offender.

DISCUSSION QUESTIONS

1. What is the definition for retreat?

2. Do you have to be close to the person you have reconciled with?

3. Will the offender that you reconcile with always respond favorably?

4. How did Jacob respond to Esau's invitation to live with him in Seir?

5. How did David respond to Saul's violence?

6. What should you do with a person who repeatedly offends you?

7. How do you know when you have made the right decision with an offender?

CHAPTER 6

Bury The Past To Birth The Present

—◆—

Revelation 21:4 (ESV)
"He will wipe away every tear from their eyes, and death shall be no more, neither shall there be mourning, nor crying, nor pain anymore, for the former things have passed away."

This is speaking of the new heaven and the new earth. The earth's system and life cycle as we know it will no longer exist. There will be no death only eternal life. Why? The old has passed away.

2 Corinthians 5:17 (ESV)
"Therefore, if anyone is in Christ, he is a new creation. The old has passed away; behold, the new has come."

You are a new creation in Christ. Not will be, you are! The old you, meaning the sinful nature, was buried with Christ. The new you came forth with Him in His resurrection.

Romans 6:3–4 (ESV)
"Do you not know that all of us who have been baptized into Christ Jesus were baptized into his death? We were buried therefore with him by baptism into death, in order that, just as Christ was raised from the dead by the glory of the Father, we too might walk in newness of life."

You are walking in newness of life.

THE PAIN WILL END WHEN YOU ALLOW THE PAST TO DIE

For something new to begin the old must die. A seed in the ground must die to bring forth new fruit. The old covenant had to pass away for the new covenant to be established.

Paul uses the analogy of marriage to deal with this subject.

Romans 7:2 (ESV)
"For a married woman is bound by law to her husband while he lives, but if her husband dies she is released from the law of marriage."

In other words, the woman is free to marry again when her husband dies. Are you willing to allow the past to die? How can this be done? What does it look like?

Starve The Past

It is like a plant being plucked or pulled up (Ecclesiastes 3:2). A plant cannot grow outside of the soil. The roots will wither and the plant dies. Why? It has nothing from which to draw nutrients. It is starved to death. Your mind is the soil. The plant is pain from the events of your past. The roots are the thoughts that remind you of the past.

A person asked me once, "I have sown so much sin in my past. I know that I will reap what I sow. What can I do that will help me to overcome what I have done?" This person was filled with remorse and regret. The harvest of past actions, like a boomerang, was coming back in this person's life.

I believe the Lord gave me a word that would help this person. I said, "Sow more righteous acts in your future than the sinful acts you have sown in your past. The latter harvests will overpower the former harvest. The sins of the flesh are like weeds but the many acts of righteousness are seeds of abundance that will choke out the weeds of the past."

We have a promise from God's Word that we can reap a better harvest. You determine which is the larger harvest.

Galatians 6:8–9 (ESV)
"For the one who sows to his own flesh will from the flesh reap corruption, but the one who sows to the Spirit will from the Spirit reap eternal life. And let us not grow weary of doing good, for in due season we will reap, if we do not give up."

Take Your Focus Off Of The Past

Jesus uses a hyperbole in addressing how to deal with the tendency of the eyes to sin.

Mark 9:47 (NKJV)
"And if your eye causes you to sin, pluck it out. It is better for you to enter the kingdom of God with one eye, rather than having two eyes, to be cast into hell fire—"

The point He is making is concerning where the eye is focused. He is teaching that if you can't control your focus pluck out your eye as a means of avoiding sin that would put you in hell.

The method Jesus is teaching is to sever, separate, or remove what causes you to be tempted to sin. The same principle applies to the thoughts that are in your mind. If you continually focus your spiritual eye on the things of the past you are allowing the issues of the past to take root and to continue to live. You alone determine what you dwell on. You have the power according to the Word of God to cast down every thought. Stop giving life to the past!

To live in the present and have hope for your future, you cannot continue to focus on your past life. If you do, your life will be a struggle. Jesus said, "Remember Lot's wife!" She was given an instruction that would save her future.

Genesis 19:17 (ESV)
"And as they brought them out, one said, 'Escape for your life. Do not look back or stop anywhere in the valley. Escape to the hills, lest you be swept away.'"

Foolishly she did not obey the warning of the angel; she looked back. Perhaps she looked back because she had two sons-in-law who remained in the city. She had a home there. It was a prosperous place. It was a beautiful place. Her husband was on the city council. She was leaving her past behind. Just one glance backward and she lost her life. She became a standing pillar of salt. Jesus would use her story to be a warning, "Remember Lot's wife!"

What are we to learn from her? Leave the past behind you and don't look back. Your future is in front of you. Don't sacrifice the blessings of your future by continually focusing on the past. **You destroy expectation of a**

better life by being consumed with what you cannot change.

Joseph is a classic example of how to deal with the pain of the past. His brothers hate him because of his father's favoritism. They sell him as a slave and tell Jacob an animal has killed him. He ends up in prison for a false accusation of attempting to rape his master's wife. Eventually, he fulfills his destiny. He becomes second to the king of Egypt, by interpreting his dream.

He marries and has children. The name of his firstborn gives us insight to how God has helped him with his past.

Genesis 41:51 (ESV)
"Joseph called the name of the firstborn Manasseh. 'For,' he said, 'God has made me forget all my hardship and all my father's house.'"

How is that possible? Joseph had a relationship with God that brought continual favor in his life. He is placed over Potiphar's house. When in prison he is placed over the prisoners. When he is presented to the king of Egypt he is placed over Egypt.

His faith was in the God of his dreams. His attitude was to serve. He realized his destiny and the fulfillment of his childhood dreams when he was elevated next to the king.

We should learn from him that whatever family, friends, or people do to us they do not have the power to alter our destiny. When he says that God has made him forget the hardship it is because he is now living out his life's purpose. He is blessed and highly favored.

Genesis 45:4–8 (NKJV)
"And Joseph said to his brothers, 'Please come near to me.' So they came near. Then he said: 'I am Joseph your brother, whom you sold into Egypt. But now, do not therefore be grieved or angry with yourselves because you sold me here; for God sent me before you to preserve life. For these two years the famine has been in the land, and there are still five years in which there will be neither plowing nor harvesting. And God sent me before you to preserve a posterity for you in the earth, and to save your lives by a great deliverance. So now it was not you who sent me here, but God; and He has made me a father to Pharaoh, and lord of all his house, and a ruler throughout all the land of Egypt.'"

Joseph buried his past to give birth to the present. He could forget because he had forgiven his brothers.

"You will never understand how God uses evil for good until you forgive." –Tony Evans

The character of Joseph was developed in his suffering. His suffering ended when he reached his place of his destiny, the palace.

REALIZE THE WORK OF GRACE IN YOUR PRESENT

Don't focus on what was or could have been. Focus on what is and what can be by the grace of God. The fulfillment of where God is taking you will cause the pain of the past to diminish.

Grace is not for the past, nor the future. It is for the present.

2 Corinthians 12:9 (ESV)
"But he said to me, 'My grace is sufficient for you, for my power is made perfect in weakness.' Therefore I will boast all the more gladly of my weaknesses, so that the power of Christ may rest upon me."

1 Corinthians 16:23 (ESV)
"The grace of the Lord Jesus be with you."

Joseph could forget because he was so greatly blessed in his present. Have you allowed yourself to become so oppressed that you can't see what God is doing in your present? Stop and count your blessings. All has not been lost.

This passage of Scripture will help you to see what God has done and is doing in your life now.

Psalm 103:1–5 (KJV)
"Bless the LORD, O my soul:
And all that is within me, *bless* his holy name.
Bless the LORD, O my soul,
And forget not all his benefits:
Who forgiveth all thine iniquities;
Who healeth all thy diseases;
Who redeemeth thy life from destruction;
Who crowneth thee with lovingkindness and tender mercies;
Who satisfieth thy mouth with good *things*;
So that thy youth is renewed like the eagle's."

Read this out loud to yourself. Stop right now and just begin to thank Him for what He has done and praise Him for what He is going to do.

REJOICE THAT THE PRESENT IS ESTABLISHING YOUR FUTURE

Joseph could rejoice because of the divine providence of God that had placed him over the king's entire wealth. He could rejoice because he had a wife to comfort him. He could rejoice because God had given him a son!

He names him Manasseh because not only has he forgotten the hardships of his past and the pain of rejection from his brothers, but now he has a future in his son!

God has a plan for your life starting at the moment of salvation.

Jeremiah 29:11 (NLT)
"'For I know the plans I have for you,' says the Lord. 'They are plans for good and not for disaster, to give you a future and a hope.'"

God's plan for you is not to continue to be the victim but the overcomer. His plan for you is to give you a dream for your future. The pain that Joseph experienced was because he had a dream. His pain came from those who did not have a dream.

You are free to dream. You are free to fulfill your destiny. Let the past and its pain die! God will keep your dream alive.

Your future is determined by whom you choose to believe.

Are you going to choose to listen to the voices of your past that have spoken curses over your life? Are you going to listen to the voice from the past that has belittled your potential? Are you listening to the voice from the past that questioned your worth? Are you going give an ear to the voice that says you don't deserve to be loved? Are you going to believe the voice that says you are only good to be used?

There is a voice in the present that is speaking to you! Let the past die! It is not who you are. It is saying you are mighty through God to the pulling down of strongholds. It is saying that you are righteous. It is saying you can do all things through Christ who strengthens you. It is speaking that no weapon formed against you is going to succeed. It is declaring that you are one of God's chosen. It is saying that you have power to cast out devils in His name. It is saying that you are a child of God that is worthy of having a place at His table! Listen to that voice! That is who you are. You are not dead you are alive!

The Father refuses to allow you to be trapped in the past. His focus is now. When the prodigal son returns home he declares for all to hear, "This my son was dead, and is alive again; he was lost, and is found." (Luke 15:24).

His son would not be known for his past, he would be known for his present.

Notice how the father establishes his new identity. He is given new clothes. The clothes of his past had the smell of a pigpen. It was most insulting to Jewish culture. Those clothes identified him to loss and sinful activity. The order was to give him the best robe! This identified him with family. Only family wore the best robes. It was a symbol of new life. It was a symbol of the beginning of a new future.

Your identity is established when the Father clothes you in a robe of righteousness. It is His righteousness not your own.

The servant is told to put a ring on his finger. That ring was a signet ring. It was a ring of authority. It gave him access to the family treasure. What he had lost was being restored.

Shoes were placed on his feet. This implied ownership. Slaves did not wear shoes. He was completely validated as a worthy son.

Everything in his life changed when he came back to the father. He asked for forgiveness and received grace. His shame was covered with the robe identifying him as a son. His poverty was replaced by the father's provision. His bare feet were a testimony of his past as a slave. Now the father places shoes on his feet that had been removed because of his past activity. All he once had, he had now lost. At the father's house, all loss is replaced.

A spiritual daughter, Julie Ballard, gave me insight to loss when she said, "I measured my life by loss and I always came up short. The only thing left after loss is pain." This is her testimony of how the Lord restored her loss.

> *"One of my earliest memories of childhood is the loss of my sister. My mother sank into depression, while my father sank into addiction. They both forgot about the living. When she died I felt like I not only lost a sibling, but my childhood as well.*
>
> *Many things taught me to measure my life by loss. My parents' inability to cope with their own pain became the cause of mine through abuse at the hands and the words of my Father. His destructive words and actions distorted not only my own identity, but also the way I saw God as a father.*
>
> *The early loss of innocence led me into an addictive lifestyle. Lacking in family stability I*

searched for my identity through empty relationships. Loss was something that I simply just
expected, because it was all I knew.

In what would be one of the lowest moments
of my life, I felt the Lord draw on my heart. I
started attending church with the man who is
now my husband. I had no idea how drastical-
ly not only my life was about to change, but
the lives of my two sons. Or what that change
would bring to my future.

Shortly after attending I went through Emotional
Healing. Through that process God began to
heal the wounds of my past. I was now able to
have memories, but without pain. Becoming
pain free allowed me to see past loss, and live
with expectation.

After healing took place, I could now trust. My
pastor would become my spiritual father. As
that relationship developed, God used it to restore my identity, and give me a healthy con-
cept of Father God. In the past I struggled with
wrong relationships. Now God was using that
one right relationship to change the course of
my entire life. It would restore everything that
had been lost.

I could see me according to what the Word of God says about me. Not the words of an angry earthly father, but the words of my Heavenly Father. When I looked in the mirror I could see a woman who was called to preach not live in shame. I am no longer shaped by the words or opinions of others. I am free because I have buried my past.

*The ministry that I received healing from now has become my passion. God has given me an anointing to set people free from the very things I once struggled with. Where there was once a lack of identity now it has become my platform from which to speak. I no longer measure my life by what I've lost, but what I've gained through Christ."— **Julie Ballard***

In the present the Father is restoring and replacing what has been taken from you. He is giving you a clean slate. It is a new beginning. Your life now is like Noah and his family who stepped out of the ark after the world's greatest flood. Their past was buried beneath the turbulent waters. They felt they had lost everything. All they had was each other and the animals that were in the ark. How would they survive?

They would survive because there is life in a seed. When God told them to build the ark, and store food for themselves and the animals, He did not give them an instruction to store seed. The precious seed of life remained in the earth.

Seed is God's way of perpetuating life in man, animals, and plants. The flood destroyed everything but seed. Seed has the power to always produce its own kind.

The storm of your past that has left you loss and pain no longer exists. You may feel that all is lost. You may see your future as barren flooded earth. Wait! You will recover what has been lost. You have the seed of God's Word. You are good soil. The seed of God's Word is in you and He is going to germinate it or quicken it by the Holy Spirit. You may think there is nothing in you but you have eternal life. You are going to see the barrenness of your past life replaced by blessing, favor, grace, goodness, and prosperity.

- You can get your family back.
- You can get your home back.
- You can get your health back.
- You can get your wealth back.
- You can get your life back.
- You can get your mind back.
- You can get your joy back.
- You can get your innocence back.
- You can get your reputation back.

The seed of God's Word is breaking forth to give you a blessed future.

Noah received a sign of promise that the past would not return. It was the rainbow. **God has given you a sign that the past will not return. It is the cross.**

2 Corinthians 5:17 (ESV)
"Therefore, if anyone is in Christ, he is a new creation. The old has passed away; behold, the new has come."

DISCUSSION QUESTIONS

1. When does the pain cease?

2. When something new is to be established what must happen first?

3. How do you allow the past to die?

4. How is the past like a plant?

5. Why is Lot's wife to be remembered?

6. How was Joseph able to forget his past?

7. When is grace functional?

8. How did the father remove the prodigal's past?

9. What did God leave Noah to survive with after the flood?

10. What sign did God give Noah that the past would not repeat itself?

11. What sign has God given us that our past is removed?

CHAPTER 7

Rehabilitate to Recover

———◆———

MY COUSIN, DAVID AND HIS wife, Christi were in a tragic motorcycle accident recently. David went to be with the Lord. Christi was severely injured and hospitalized for three months. Before being released from the hospital she had to learn to do the simplest of tasks. Every muscle needed to be exercised. Every nerve was extremely sensitive to the exercise. Rehabilitation was a must for her body to be restored to normal body functions.

The same is true with healing of damaged emotions. Though the healing is taking place there must be caution with the recovery process. Don't attempt to have relationships instantly restored. True recovery requires time. Enter back into relationships slowly and wisely.

Rehabilitation requires the proper training. You must have proper instruction concerning the limits of your exercise. It is important to know how much exercise is beneficial and know when the exercise becomes detrimental to the process. This principle also applies to you recovering from damaged emotions.

I recommend that you exercise these four basic principles to help your spiritual rehabilitation. These will speed up the healing process.

1. Apply the Word of God.

Never minimize the power of the Word of God. It has the power to heal.

Psalm 107:19–20 (ESV)
"Then they cried to the Lord in their trouble,
and he delivered them from their distress.
He sent out his word and healed them,
and delivered them from their destruction."

The Word of God is like a double-edged sword that has the power to divide the soul and the spirit. It can penetrate your thoughts and intentions.

Hebrews 4:12 (ESV)
"For the word of God is living and active, sharper than any two-edged sword, piercing to the division of soul and of spirit, of joints and of marrow, and discerning the thoughts and intentions of the heart."

His words are spirit and life.

John 6:63 (ESV)
"It is the Spirit who gives life; the flesh is no help at all. The words that I have spoken to you are spirit and life."
The Word of God helps you to withstand the enemy's attack by re-establishing your faith in God and yourself. It is the stabilizing force that keeps you from falling.

Psalm 119:85–89 (ESV)
"The insolent have dug pitfalls for me;
they do not live according to your law.
All your commandments are sure;
they persecute me with falsehood; help me!
They have almost made an end of me on earth,
but I have not forsaken your precepts.
In your steadfast love give me life,
that I may keep the testimonies of your mouth.
Forever, O Lord, your word
is firmly fixed in the heavens."

The Word of God is like a salve on your broken heart and wounded spirit. It will heal the emotional pain that has been a stronghold in your life.

It is time to move. No more mourning, crying, and pleading. Instead of asking God to do something for us acknowledge, through Christ, the powerful Spirit and Word of God. He is the Word. He watches over it to perform it. He has placed His Word above His name. Apply it. It will work for you.

2. RE-ESTABLISH YOUR PRAYER LIFE.

Daniel was a man who dealt with a lot of emotional issues, yet established himself with greatness. His secret was his prayer life.

As a young man he was taken from his home to a land far away, Babylon. It was a different culture. He had to learn a different language. They changed his name in an attempt to change his identity. They emasculated him. He would be a eunuch for life. He would never have children. It is not recorded that he ever married. If that was not enough, when he begins advancing among the leadership of the nation, jealous souls passed a law stating that anyone found praying would be punished by death.

These are overwhelming, emotional issues that would cause anyone to quit.

Daniel did not adhere to it. What made Daniel great was what got him into trouble and is the same thing that got him out of trouble. Prayer. He continued as he always had praying three times a day toward Jerusalem with his window open.

Not backing down from his edict the king has Daniel thrown into a den of hungry lions. It would not deter Daniel's destiny. They king inquires if he is alive. Daniel affirms that he is and that the Lord has sent an angel to close the mouths of the lions.

Daniel 6:22 (ESV)
"My God sent his angel and shut the lions' mouths, and they have not harmed me, because I was found blameless before him; and also before you, O king, I have done no harm."

Prayer is conversation with God. When you pray believe that what He has done for you He is able to safeguard. He did not heal your emotions to relapse. The all-powerful God has limited His action to your prayer. If Daniel found it necessary to pray three times a day over his issues perhaps you could receive more through prayer.

3. RE-ASSESS YOUR FRIENDSHIPS

You are not the same person of your past. You are walking in your God-given identity, free of pain. As you walk in this new identity old friends will leave you. Because you are free, your presence now makes them uncomfortable. Don't change who you are now for people who don't even know themselves. Your difference will point out their sameness. Your difference requires they make changes to remain in fellow-ship with you. Anyone who walks out of your life was not intended to be a part of your future.

"Not everyone will make it to your future. Some people are just passing through to teach you lessons in life!" – **Rick Godwin**

Most assuredly, a close friend or family member caused the pain in your past. It is most probable those who have hurt you in the past will do so again. You must determine at what level you want these people to be in your life. Though you have forgiven them it may not be wise to give them unlimited access to you. There are some that you must guard yourself by erasing messages, deleting phone numbers, and blocking calls. Eliminate all avenues of contact.

The change in you that will cause some friends to leave will attract new friends. As you begin to love yourself watch the number of your friends increase because you are real.

Your future is not tied to those who walk away but to those who have decided to enter your life. God is going to add some amazing people to your life. They will seek you out because of your difference.

You choose the friends and relationships in your life. Show me who your friends are and I will predict your future. Your future successes or failures are based on those you choose to be in your inner circle. You take on the nature of those you associate with.

+ Thieves keep company with thieves.
+ Addicts keep company with addicts.
+ Critics keep company with other critics.
+ Optimists keep company with optimists.
+ A person of faith keeps company with others of faith.
+ A person of wisdom keeps company with the wise.

To live the pain free life qualify the people who are in your inner circle. Your inner circle will always be there for you. The more that qualify for your inner circle the stronger you will be. Learn from David's experience.

David is in the cave of Adullum hiding from Saul and his army. Men were drawn to him because they knew he was real. David developed an army of thirty mighty men. Out of the thirty were three that were known as the elite of the elite. They were Josheb-basshebeth, a Tahchemonite, Eleazar, the son of Dodo and Shammah, and the son of Agee the Hararite.

David was thirsty and muttered to himself how he would love to have a drink from the well in Bethlehem. These men heard it and risked their lives to meet his desire. When they returned having successfully evaded the enemy, they presented it to David. He was so overwhelmed by the honor and effort of these men to satisfy his thirst that he poured it out on the ground as an offering to the Lord.

You have friends at three levels.

1. Perimeter – They are on the outer fringe.
2. Acquaintances – These are people you like, but they couldn't tell you your birthday, or any other personal things about you.
3. Inner circle- They are there because you respect them and they respect you.

Jesus had the multitude, the 500, the 120, the 70, the 12, and the 3. These relationships ranged from the outer edge of those who knew of Him to those who knew Him intimately.

SEVEN CHARACTERISTICS OF THOSE WHO QUALIFY TO BE IN YOUR INNER CIRCLE

1. Unconditional love

This person does not want what you have. They do not want to use you for a stepping-stone to advance them. They love you for being you. They love you at your best and at your worst. They know your faults and choose to love you in spite of them. They meet the biblical definition of a friend.

Proverbs 17:17 (NKJV)
"A friend loves at all times."

This person will give their life for you. There is no greater love than a man that will lay down his life for his friend.

2. Honesty

You must have someone who loves you enough to tell you the truth. This person will hold you accountable to what you say and do. They may say:
"You need a break! You are pushing too much."
"You were wrong when you did this."
"You are getting too big for your britches!"

You know that they will always speak the truth in love to you. You know that their intention is to make you better not to hurt your feelings.

3. Protector (Armor bearer)

This person stands between you and your enemy. They have your back. They will not allow people near you that will hurt you with words or physical harm. They warn you of danger points in your life. They refuse to allow you to be vulnerable to bad relationships, temptation, or undue criticism. This person makes you feel safe.

4. Encouraging

We all want an encourager like Jonathan. Jonathan, the son of King Saul, was the man who would encourage David when he was overwhelmed by the anger of Saul. Five times Saul would attempt to kill David. In those moments when his life was threatened his closest friend Jonathan would come to him to encourage him that he would someday be king. Though he himself was in line to be king he recognized the hand of God on David. He would enter into a covenant with David that he would show kindness to his descendants when he became king. He could encourage David because of his love for him.

When Saul of Tarsus was converted the church was afraid of him because of his past. No one would befriend him but Barnabas. His name means 'encourager'. He would do ministry with Saul when no one else would. He would be the one to take him to the church leadership and confirm his message to the Gentiles. He would be the person who would avow that Saul was now Paul, a changed man.

You need someone who encourages you when your past is in question.

King David flees the city of Jerusalem because of the insurrection of his son Absalom. After Absalom has been killed David is returning in mourning and wondering if the people would want him to continue being their king. A man named Barzillai meets him with food and friendship. No one else came to encourage him during his personal loss and displacement but this man.

5. Attentive Listener

We all need someone to listen. This friend wants to listen. They hear your heart. They hear things in your conversation that others do not hear. They not only hear but they understand.

They do not offer advice. They do not anticipate nor interrupt what you're sharing with them. You are free to express dreams, visions, personal goals, temptations, joy, sorrows, grief, joys, fears, anger, etc. You know that what you are saying will not be repeated through "the grapevine."

They do not condemn you for your thoughts or the attitude in which you expressed them. They offer no correction. They do not judge you. They listen to share the moment. What you feel, they feel. This person is a treasure. You do not want to lose this person out of your life.

6. Loyalty

David was loyal to Saul when Saul pursued him. Even though he attempted to kill David five times David was loyal to him. When David had opportunity to kill him he would not because he was God's anointed. When Saul dies David mourns him greatly.

Why was he loyal? Saul is family. He was his father-in-law. He gave him his first wife. Also, if Saul had not given him favor he would not be where he was. Even though Saul was not loyal to David, he was to Saul.

This friend will not betray you. He will be with you through the good and the bad. **We all need a friend like Silas who will take a beating with us and then sing with us all night!**

7. Trust

A person that you could give your wallet to and go home to a sound sleep is a person you can trust. If you can trust people with money you can trust them with almost anything. Many of the parables that Jesus taught concerning stewardship dealt with the principle of trust. The love of money is the root of all evil.

There is always the risk of a Judas among your friends. When the money is on the table he will reach for it. He will sell you out for the right price. He is the one that uses you for his personal benefit. He is a betrayer.

Judas was not the only one who betrayed Jesus. The other disciples did also. Yet Jesus knew them. He knew what was in their hearts. After His crucifixion and resurrection what He had taught them and what they had seen Him do inspired them to lay down their lives for Him.

If a friend exhibits the seven previous qualities in your relationship, he is a friend you can trust.

Who is the person that you would go into battle with?

Buck Trent, a former banjo player in the late Porter Wagner's band, while being interviewed on a television show was asked, "What kind of man was Porter Watner?" Buck's response was, "If I had one man to go into battle with, Porter would be that man."

This is the person you want in your life. This is the person you want to be in others' lives. To know that you have earned someone's trust at that level is the ultimate in friendship.

4. CHANGE YOUR ENVIRONMENT.

When recovering from a surgery, the healing process requires the right environment. You have special people assigned to you to make sure you are cared for properly. They are very attentive to the environment, making sure everything is sanitized. Even visitors have limited access during rehabilitation.

The same diligence given to treat physical injury is necessary for healing emotional and spiritual pain. Living the pain free life requires that you change your environment. The environment of your past has been filled with darkness of fear, anger, bitterness, and despair. It has been stagnated with the stale air of confinement. You chose your environment. You can't recover in an environment that prevents you from feeling good about yourself.

It is time to make the necessary changes in your environment that induce healing, new life, and expectancy.

Living the pain free life requires that you be surrounded with an environment of peace.

Isaiah 32:17–18 (ESV)
"And the effect of righteousness will be peace,
and the result of righteousness, quietness and trust forever.
My people will abide in a peaceful habitation,
in secure dwellings, and in quiet resting places."

Damaged emotions and nerves that have been on edge must find a quiet place. Avoid the hustle and bustle. Seek tranquility.

In Psalm twenty-three David gives us a picture of tranquility and peace playing a part in the restoration process. He mentions sheep lying down in green pastures and drinking from calm waters. There is something about animals, green grass, and water that are calming to look at. David went on to say, "He restores my soul." The soul is the seat of our emotions. Before getting back into the stresses of life allow your mind to settle and begin to allow your emotions to recover.

It is imperative that the effects of anger, fear, jealousy, and physical violation be allowed to heal in a peaceful environment. You must find a place where you can go to shut down, to get away from the noise and the stresses of life. You will literally feel the stress lifting off of you as you allow yourself to relax.

Peace is a key to rest.

Psalm 4:8 (NKJV)
"I will both lie down in peace, and sleep;
For You alone, O LORD, make me dwell in safety."

What is the source of joy?

Psalm 16:11 (ESV)
"In your presence there is fullness of joy."

The environment of the kingdom of God is the environment that will heal your soul. Righteousness produces an atmosphere of peace.

Romans 14:17 (NKJV)
"For the kingdom of God is not eating and drinking, but righteousness and peace and joy in the Holy Spirit."

Righteousness produces peace, and peace produces joy.

Proverbs 12:20 (ESV)
"Those who plan peace have joy."

Did you notice the intentionality that produces joy? You must deliberately plan an environment that produces peace. Make it happen. Whatever it takes. The reward will be joy.

An environment of joy allows the soul to heal. Surround yourself with joyful people. Your spirits will lift. The darkness is penetrated with the light of joy and you will begin to see things differently. Absorb all the joy you can. It is a medicine that adds to your wholeness.

Proverbs 17:22 (ESV)
"A joyful heart is good medicine, but a crushed spirit dries up the bones."

"Find a place where there's joy, and the joy will burn out the pain" **–Joseph Campbell**

The Scriptures are replete with opportunities for the atmosphere of joy to be experienced and expressed. One such way is music. Music has the power to reach the inner part of man. We are told to create sounds of joy with musical instruments.

1 Chronicles 15:16 (ESV)
"David also commanded the chiefs of the Levites to appoint their brothers as the singers who should play loudly on musical instruments, on harps and lyres and cymbals, to raise sounds of joy."

Hospitals use music and sounds to calm the emotional state of the patient. The result being healing occurs more rapidly.

In the Psalms David encourages us to make a joyful noise to the Lord, to shout for joy (because of our salvation or deliverance), and to dance for joy. These are all demonstrations of joy. Don't you think it is about time to free your healed emotions and begin to experience the joy of the Lord in this manner?

If you want spiritual rehabilitation, allow the joy of the Lord to be your strength.

Nehemiah 8:10 (ESV)
"For the joy of the LORD is your strength."

Joy is a fruit of the Spirit (Galatians 5:22). Because the Holy Spirit resides in you, joy is abundantly available. He will fill you full of joy (Acts 13:52). How does He fill you with joy?

John 15:9–11 (KJV)
"As the Father hath loved me, *so have I loved you*: continue ye in my love. If ye keep my commandments, ye shall *abide in my love*; even as I have kept my Father's commandments, and abide in his love. These things have *I spoken unto you, that my joy might remain in you,* and *that your joy might be full."*

Receive His words of love and be filled with the joy they bring. The joy He gives is a joy that remains.

Joy produces hope. Out of joy arises expectation. You are hopeful that something good is happening in your life.

Romans 15:13 (ESV)
"May the God of hope fill you with all joy and peace in believing, so that by the power of the Holy Spirit you may abound in hope."

When David becomes king, he is overwhelmed by the elaborate blessings of the Lord. He is so blessed he wants to bless a son or descendant of Saul. Follow the progression of how God moves a man from despair to blessing.

2 Samuel 9:3–5 (ESV)
"And the king said, 'Is there not still someone of the house of Saul, that I may show the kindness of God to him?' Ziba said to the king, 'There is still a son of Jonathan; he is crippled in his feet.' The king said to him, 'Where is he?' And Ziba said to the king, 'He is in the house of Machir the son of Ammiel, at Lo-debar.' Then King David sent and brought him from the house of Machir the son of Ammiel, at Lo-debar."

Let's examine this story a little more in depth. Saul's grandson's name is Mephibosheth. His name means, "Confusion; shame; shameful. From my mouth shame."

We learn he also is a cripple. When he was a baby his nurse dropped him as they were fleeing from an enemy, leaving him lame the rest of his life. Notice also that he lived in Lo-debar. Lo-debar means "without pasture."

Now let's put this altogether. Mephibosheth is Saul's grandson by Jonathan, David's best friend. He is a king's kid that is crippled in an accident. His grandfather dies in shame from suicide. He leaves the palace and ends up in Lo-debar a place that is barren and not productive.

It is there the messengers of David invite him to an audience with the king. I am certain that when he received this order to appear before the king his thoughts ran away with him. He probably thought, "He is going to kill me because I am heir to the throne of King Saul."

To his great surprise, David greets him and blesses him.

2 Samuel 9:7 (ESV)
"And David said to him, 'Do not fear, for I will show you kindness for the sake of your father Jonathan, and I will restore to you all the land of Saul your father, and you shall eat at my table always.'"

David blesses him with his grandfather's inheritance! But that is not the greatest blessing. He receives his honor back. David said, "You shall eat at my table always." As long as David lived, Mephibosheth would have a place at his family table!

Mephibosheth lives up to his name. He sees himself as shameful and unworthy because of his physical condition.

2 Samuel 9:8 (ESV)
"And he paid homage and said, 'What is your servant, that you should show regard for a dead dog such as I?'"

When he called himself a dead dog he was saying that he was less than a man.

2 Samuel 9:11–12 (ESV)
"So Mephibosheth ate at David's table, like one of the king's sons. And Mephibosheth had a young son, whose name was Mica."

After David has restored him back to his honorable place, and he is having daily fellowship with David at his table, something amazing takes place.

Wow! Do you see it? Mephibosheth has a young son whose name was Mica. Mica means, "Who is like Jehovah". Apparently, he had no son until David came into his life.

David gave Mephibosheth hope. Look what hope produces! When one who considers himself a "dead dog" receives *hope* for his future, he *produces life*.

When you have rehabilitated and recovered from the wounds of your past you are standing on the same ground as Mephibosheth. His story is your story. You saw yourself in shame, worthless, and hopeless. When Jesus invited you to fellowship with Him at His table, He reveals to you who you are; you're a king's kid. He has restored what has been taken from you. He blessed you with an inheritance. He has blessed you with His presence!

Now you have hope. You are going to give birth to a future filled with blessing! You are going to be a producer.

Discussion Questions

1. At what levels does the Word of God heal?

2. What emotional pain did Daniel have to overcome by prayer?

3. Why do you need to reassess your friends?

4. What are the qualifications of friendship to be in your inner circle?

5. What are the 3 levels of friends?

6. What role did Jonathan play in David's life?

7. What is the required environment for healing to take place?

8. What did hope do for Mephibosheth?

CHAPTER 8

Free to Love

———◆———

LOVE IS ESSENTIAL TO LIFE. Maia Szalavitz said, "When an infant falls below the threshold of physical affection needed to stimulate the production of growth hormone and the immune system, his body starts shutting down." Further evidence indicates that lack of touch and affection in early life reduces I.Q. and increases risk of behavioral and psychological problems.

Love is the greatest healing agent on the planet! If I can help you understand love, the emotional pain you are experiencing will immediately begin to heal.

Most songs are inspired by it. Wars have been fought over it. Many have attempted to explain it. May I just say that love is intended to be experienced? There is a deep longing in every person to love and be loved.

The pain began when you felt that you were not loved. You instead had feelings of rejection. You have never felt you were good enough. Longing to be loved and accepted you yielded your will to the will of others. Like wet clay, whenever pressure has been applied in your life you have yielded to it. You look into the mirror and you see yourself as a distorted lump of clay. Inwardly you ask yourself, "Why can't people accept me for who I am? Why do people want to change me? Why can't people just love me for who I really am?" All you have ever wanted in your life is to be loved and accepted.

Has your life been a cycle of repeated rejection? Are you afraid of love? Are you afraid of being hurt in a personal relationship? Do you feel unworthy of being celebrated? When love is expressed to you does it feel awkward? Is love something you desperately desire but don't know how to receive or respond to?

I minister to people weekly who have no understanding of what love is. Because they have been deprived of love, they have no more feelings for a person than they would for a tree. They see people as objects. They struggle understanding the love of a father and more specifically the love of God the Father. Before I can take them through an emotional healing session I give them assignments to study the love of God and how to understand the nature and heart of God.

Love is frustrating to them. They are ambiguous and ambivalent about what love is supposed to feel like. The following questions and observations are not intended to be offensive. I am talking about extreme cases not the average relationship with a pet. I have noticed that a person who has not been shown love may love their pets more than people. Why? They can't talk back. They don't reject them. A pet becomes the object of their love because they have a need not just to be loved, but to give love without reservation.

Do you cry more over the death of an animal or the pain of an animal than you do the death of a human? Is it easy for you to say, "I love you," to a pet but you struggle saying it to a human? Do you tell your pet secrets that you wouldn't dare tell a person? Are you alone with your pets more than with people or family?

I have often been asked, with deep sincerity, if pets are going to be in heaven. My response is that we know there are animals in heaven. If that is what it takes for you to be happy, they will be there. There is no sorrow in heaven. They are more concerned about their pet's being in heaven than a person being in heaven.

Don't take me wrong. I am not in opposition to having pets. Two-thirds of Americans have a pet. They are such fun and bring comfort and healing to so many. I have had pets and loved them. I wept over them when they died. I felt the loss of the joy that they once gave me. The people

I am writing about seem to have a much deeper attachment than just being a pet lover.

The question I ask is, "Why would a person love a pet equally to or more than people?"

While doing emotional healing sessions in another country I witnessed a very unusual healing. My team was dealing with a young man, I will call Jack, in his thirties who had experienced severe rejection all of his life. He spent most of his time alone with his dog. His best friend was his dog. Wherever he went his dog followed. This dog was his *only* friend.

When he was nine he was walking down the street and his dog ventured into the street. He was run over by a vehicle and died. In a moment of panic people inquired, "Who's dog is this?" Jack was so shocked and traumatized that when he wanted to speak he couldn't. When he did speak, it came out with a stutter, "He is, he is, he is, my, my, my, dog!" From that day forward Jack stuttered.

The team ministered to his emotional pain with the Word of God. He was taught the love of God, how to grieve, to love others, and to love himself. While he was being taught, and acting on what he had learned, he began to speak clearly for the first time since he was nine! He was healed by the power of love. God cared so deeply about the grief he had from losing his pet that He gave him a greater love than he had ever experienced before, the love of his Father.

Regardless of whether you have not known love or had love and lost it, if you do not love you will live a miserable life. **When you refuse to love, you are empty.**

Paul explains it in 1 Corinthians 13:1-3 (NKJV), "Though I speak with the tongues of men and of angels, but have not love, I have become sounding brass or a clanging cymbal. And though I have *the gift of* prophecy, and understand all mysteries and all knowledge, and though I have all faith, so that I could remove mountains, but *have not love, I am nothing.* And though I bestow all my goods to feed *the poor,* and though I give my body to be burned, but *have not love, it profits me nothing.*"

Paul describes this emptiness in these words, "have not love, I am nothing." He goes on to say that any spiritual exercise or generosity offered without love leaves one empty.

Love is the greatest gift you can give or will ever receive.

1 Corinthians 13:13 (NKJV)
"And now abide faith, hope, love, these three; but the greatest of these *is* love."

Teffany was a young lady I was privileged to pastor for a very short season. She was in her mid-twenties and had four lovely children. Her life took a very hard turn when she was diagnosed with cancer. I have never witnessed a more powerful demonstration of love than what our church gave her family.

Money was given to help with expenses. Meals were provided on a regular, scheduled basis. People would come to the church to pray for her healing. I would take a staff member two times a day to her home in the final stages to pray for her healing. A prayer vigil was called for and people made a circle around her home to pray. I personally fasted twenty-eight days asking God for her healing.

Teffany passed away. I was so set in my desire for her to be healed that I went to the funeral home and in a private setting began to pray for God to raise her from the dead. I was not prepared for what the Father would speak to me at that moment. He said, "I am pleased with all that you and your church have done for Teffany and her family. You have fasted twenty-eight days for a woman who is eternally safe in heaven but you have never fasted that long for a lost soul going to hell." Immediately I stopped praying and accepted her death.

Because our church believes in divine healing it affected the faith and spirit of the people. We so believed that she would be healed. I personally struggled over it. How could I believe God for others to be healed after this mother of four dies? We had believed for her recovery; now we questioned our faith. For a season, I was so disappointed that I lost the desire to pray for the healing of others.

My niece's husband, Derek, knowing my personal struggle of faith sent me a card in the mail that would give me great encouragement and perspective. It said, "Glenn, I know that you have had a spiritual let down over Teffany's death. While I was praying, I felt the Lord gave me a word for you. You have felt that you did not have enough faith for her to be healed. This verse came to me, 'Now abides faith, hope, and love but the greatest of these is love.' All that your church did for her and her family was greater than faith. You and your church gave them the greatest gift, love."

Wow! That changed my focus forever. Desire this gift! To *know* God is to know love.

1 John 4:8 (NKJV)
"He who does not love does not know God, for God is love."

Love is eternal because God is eternal. It is not temporary like a material object that can be destroyed. It is the very nature of God. Therefore, if God is love we know that true love emanates from having a meaningful relationship with Him. He is the source of love.

The Father created you to be loved and to love.

When the Lord called me into ministry I struggled with love. The reason being, my personal pain had come from a group of super-spiritual people that were extremely legalistic. As a pastor's son, I witnessed their hypocrisy and vicious attacks on my father. I had determined that I would never darken a church door when I left home. My father said to me, "Son, I know that you have seen and heard things from church people that you should not have heard. I want you to understand that regardless of what I have gone through I would do it again. Son, not everybody in the body of Christ is doing it wrong. Don't focus on those people. Focus on those that are doing it right." I would never forget that wisdom. I told the Lord that I would answer the call if He would teach me how to love His people. He assured me He would and He did. He would teach me to love those who hurt others.

A young man came to us on the verge of losing his family. He had been physically and verbally abused by both of his parents. His father whipped him with electrical cords and coat hangers. He would call him lazy, worthless and untrustworthy. His mother would bite and kick him. He never received praise. He could never please them.

The sad part of this story is his father was a minister. His father had been unfaithful, and would eventually leave his wife and son due to divorce.

This young man himself eventually went into the ministry. The pastor he served, like his father, would never affirm him. He would work long hours and do all he could to please the pastor but never received praise or recognition for his efforts.

The father figures in his life, his father and spiritual father, had both disappointed him. Neither of them affirmed him as man. He did not see himself as a mature man but a young immature male. Now he finds himself about to lose his family because he does not know how to love his wife and kids.

I am happy to say that when he confronted his inability to love his life changed.

He could not give what he himself had not been given. Today, he has saved his marriage and is being restored to ministry. He learned what true intimacy is and how to express it.

To enjoy a pain free life is to make the decision to give and receive love. These three words are the most meaningful words one can speak or hear, "I love you." To hear these words spoken out of sincerity adds value and worth to your life.

God the Father speaks these precious words to you today, "I love you."

John 3:16 (NKJV)
"For God so loved the world that He gave His only begotten Son, that whoever believes in Him should not perish but have everlasting life."

Two of the greatest commandments, according to Jesus, deal with love.

Matthew 22:37–39 (NKJV)
"Jesus said to him, '*You shall love the* LORD *your God with all your heart, with all your soul, and with all your mind.*' This is *the* first and great commandment. And *the* second *is* like it: '*You shall love your neighbor as yourself.*'"

You are to love the Lord first. You are to give Him all of yourself. Love holds nothing back. You may be thinking, "I am commanded to love God. How can I learn to love Him?"

You will begin to love God when you fully understand that God was the first to initiate love.

1 John 4:19 (NKJV)
"We love Him because He first loved us."

The story of the prodigal son gives us insight to a father's love.

The prodigal son has embarrassed himself and his family; he knows the only place he can be restored is his father's house. Disheveled in his appearance, broken in spirit, embarrassed by his actions, and penniless he returns to his father. His mind is filled with negative thoughts. It screams at him that his father will not allow him to return. He is tempted to turn away and go elsewhere. Yet he needs his father. How would the father respond?

When the prodigal was still a great distance away his father ran to meet him, and kissed him. The son left saying, "give me" and returned saying, "make me". While he was attempting to say he was no longer worthy to be called a son his father completely ignores the conversation. He demands that new clothes be given him to replace his rags, new shoes to be placed on his bare feet, and a ring to be placed on his finger to signify his restoration as a son.

Did he deserve it? No. Did he ask for it? No. Then what is the response of this father toward a son that has spent his inheritance on wine, women and song? He celebrates him with a great feast. He accepts him back into the family. Why? He loves him and knows that he has repented! The Father loves you in the same manner. Regardless of what you have done or what has been done to you, He continues to love you.

You need that! Your emotional pain will begin to heal when you learn to receive love, the Father's love. He celebrates you! He will not reject you. His perfect love will cast out all your fears. His love covers a multitude of sins. His love will heal your deepest hurts.

Isaiah 53:5 (NKJV)
"But He was wounded for our transgressions,
He was bruised for our iniquities;
The chastisement for our peace was upon Him,
And by His stripes we are healed."

God has bestowed His love on you *(1 John 3:1)*. The love that God has for you is without measure or limits. It is not an earned love. His love was manifested toward you at the very beginning of creation when He made man in His image. He knew you from the beginning of time and chose then to love you! He confirmed it when He sent His Son

Jesus to die for your sins. It was to restore man back into right relationship with Him.

Love desires a response. What is it? To be loved in return. You demonstrate your love for Him with obedience to His Word. Jesus said, "If you love me you will keep my commandments." God's passion is that you love Him.

How can you *know* you love Him?

1 John 3:16 (NKJV)
"By this we know love, because He laid down His life for us. And we also ought to lay down *our* lives for the brethren."

You know you love God when you love your fellowman.

1 John 4:20 (NKJV)
"If someone says, 'I love God,' and hates his brother, he is a liar; for he who does not love his brother whom he has seen, how can he love God whom he has not seen?"

Your vertical love must be horizontal as well. It is impossible to love God and not love your neighbor. The manner in which we love one another is a witness that we are His.

John 13:35 (NKJV)
"By this all will know that you are My disciples, if you have love for one another."

1 John 5:2 (NKJV)
"By this we know that *we love the children of God, when we love God* and keep His commandments."

You are to love others in the same manner that you have received it, unconditionally. This is not a suggestion. It is a commandment. One of the most difficult Scriptures to live out is the following:

Matthew 5:44 (NKJV)
"But I say to you, love your enemies, bless those who curse you, do good to those who hate you, and pray for those who spitefully use you and persecute you."

Your humanness does not permit you to love an enemy or bless someone who has cursed you. How then can you overcome the natural response to retaliate? This is an impossibility to accomplish without the power of the Holy Spirit to help you, and He will!

Romans 5:5 (NKJV)
"The love of God has been poured out in our hearts by the Holy Spirit who was given to us."

Notice love has already been poured in your heart because you have responded to the love of God. Therefore He will help you love others. The Holy Spirit will give you the power to love others, even those who have hurt you.

There is nothing that convicts me more personally than when I hear a sermon on love. I feel that this is the greatest challenge to the Christian. My life was greatly affected when God showed me my heart in this area. I understood that I was selective as to whom I was showing love. I can remember the place and the time this happened. All that Sunday afternoon I wept on the sofa over what the Lord had shown me about myself. I was so unlike Jesus. He said that if we only love those who love us we are no different than the unsaved. I only loved those who loved me but not those who were my enemies.

Matthew 5:43–44 (NKJV)
"You have heard that it was said, '*You shall love your neighbor* and hate your enemy.' But I say to you, love your enemies, bless those who curse you, do good to those who hate you, and pray for those who spitefully use you and persecute you."

Repenting of what was in my heart, I promised God that I would never again be selective about who I chose to love.

I would love *all* people. My ministry changed for the better after that day.

The second greatest commandment gives us another key to receiving and releasing love. It is "love your neighbor as yourself." This may perhaps sound vain but it is not. It is being who God has made you to be and accepting your uniqueness. It is okay to be different. You are free to love yourself because you have taken on His divine nature. That nature is to love. It is the fruit of the Spirit (Galatians 5:22).

Do you love yourself? Is it possible to love your neighbor when you don't love yourself? The fact is you can't. Your struggle with loving yourself is based on the past.

Your relationship with God through Christ changes everything about you. The process that brings this change is the word *adoption.*

Romans 8:15 (NKJV)
"For you did not receive the spirit of bondage again to fear, but you received the Spirit of adoption by whom we cry out, 'Abba, Father.'"

Recently I was in a Christian education class where adoption was being discussed. I learned some things from a couple of people in the class who had been adopted or affected by adoption. I want to share them with you.

The benefits of a biblical adoption parallel with the spiritual adoption we have in Christ. They are the following:

1. When you are adopted you begin a new life.

2 Corinthians 5:17 (NKJV)
"Therefore, if anyone *is* in Christ, *he is* a new creation;"

2. When you are adopted the records of your past are sealed.

2 Corinthians 5:17(NKJV)
"Old things have passed away; behold, all things have become new."

3. When you are adopted all debts are cancelled

Colossians 2:14 (ESV)
"By canceling the record of debt that stood against us with its legal demands. This he set aside, nailing it to the cross."

The work of the cross of Jesus was a redemptive work. His last words on the cross were, "It is finished." In the original language is a commercial term meaning "paid in full." Your sin debt has been paid. There is no longer a record of it. You come to the Father without sin's debt. You are righteous in Christ.

4. When you are adopted you receive a new Father.

God is a perfect father. Everything your earthly has not been He will be to you. He will be present. He is affirming. He loves unconditionally. He gives you his protection. He provides all of your needs. He permits failure but not sin. He desires that you spend eternity with him.

5. When you are adopted you obtain a new name.

A new name is a clear indication of disconnecting from the past and establishing a new identity. It was not uncommon in biblical days for a person to have their name changed. For example, Abram's name was changed to Abraham, Sarai to Sarah, Simon to Peter, and Saul to Paul.

I have met several believers who no longer go by their birth name, but have chosen to go by a new name because of the "new birth". They are making a clear statement, "I am not the person of my past."

Recently a young man stood and shared his testimony with the church body. He said, "Pastor asked me what my name was and I told him it was the first book of the New Testament. He said, "Matthew." I told him that was my old name. I am not the same person that started coming to church here. I thought since I gave my life to Christ and I was a new person I needed a new name. I chose the name Bear." He chose that name because he is a very large man. He wanted a new identity and he obtained it by taking on a new name.

The Father has given you a new name!

Revelation 2:17 (NKJV)
"He who has an ear, let him hear what the Spirit says to the churches. *To him who overcomes* I will give some of the hidden manna to eat. And *I will give him a white stone, and on the stone a new name written which no one knows except him who receives it.*"

The Father does not see you as you have been. He sees you as you are now and will be. Your father gives you your name. The Father has given us all a new name.

Ephesians 3:14–15 (NKJV)
"For this reason I bow my knees to the Father of our Lord Jesus Christ, from whom the whole family in heaven and earth is named."

6. When you are adopted you receive a new family.

1 John 3:1 (NKJV)
"Behold what manner of love the Father has bestowed on us, that we should be called children of God!"

7. When you are adopted you receive legal representation or an advocate.

1 John 2:1 (NKJV)
"We have an Advocate with the Father, Jesus Christ the righteous."

An advocate is legal representation to plead your case before a judge. Jesus is your Advocate. He represents you before the Father.

1 Timothy 2:5 (NKJV)
"For *there is* one God and one Mediator between God and men, *the* Man Christ Jesus."

8. When you are adopted you cannot be disinherited by your adoptive father.

You have an inheritance because of what Jesus has accomplished by the work of the cross.

1 Peter 1:3–4 (NKJV)
"Blessed *be* the God and Father of our Lord Jesus Christ, who according to His abundant mercy has begotten us again to a living hope through the resurrection of Jesus Christ from the dead, to an inheritance incorruptible and undefiled and that does not fade away, reserved in heaven for you,"

Revelation 21:7 (NKJV)
"He who overcomes shall inherit all things, and I will be his God and he shall be My son."

9. When you are adopted your new family cannot put you to death.

Remember we are dealing with biblical adoption. In that day, if a king lost his kingdom the enemy would kill those who were heirs to the throne. Some who were not royalty would attempt by death to reduce the number of siblings that would inherit family assets.

You have eternal life in Christ! You are safe in the Father's hand

John 10:28–29 (NKJV)
"And I give them eternal life, and they shall never perish; neither shall anyone snatch them out of My hand. My

Father, who has given *them* to Me, is greater than all; and no one is able to snatch *them* out of My Father's hand."

10. When you are adopted you receive a new home.

John 14:2–3 (NKJV)
"In My Father's house are many mansions; if *it were* not *so,* I would have told you. I go to prepare a place for you. And if I go and prepare a place for you, I will come again and receive you to Myself; that where I am, *there* you may be also."

11. When you are adopted you receive a generational blessing.

Before you were found in Christ, you were bound by sin and the law. You were under a generational curse of death. In Christ, you are under grace. Your ancestry may not have honored God. Now that you belong to the family of God you stepped into generational blessing. You have become an heir and a joint-heir with Jesus Christ.

Once you know the Father's love and have received it, you will be free to love yourself and then you will learn how to love others.

Love is not love if it takes. Love gives. It is no longer about your pain but that of others.

1Corinthians 13:7-8 (NKJV)
"endures all things. Love never fails."

The following testimony is that of a young lady who never knew love, but learned that love indeed "never fails."

> "I was not raised in a Christian home. The only examples of love I had as a child were selfish and destructive. I was rarely shown encouragement or physical affection. Being sexually abused further warped my views on love. This caused me to be uncomfortable in my own skin. I viewed myself as awkward because I didn't know how to respond to hugs or compliments from people in my church. In my teens, I thought that I had "gotten over it" and that none of these things affected me. I had found a church, and I was a good kid. I did well in school and didn't do drugs. I was the "poster child" in my family. In all reality, I had just never dealt with my past. I made the right choices, but on the inside I was broken and hurting.

> "I was in my twenties before I learned what true love is. Eventually, what was on the inside began to come out. I had just married my husband, and I began to be very self-destructive. I hurt everyone

around me—my friends, my husband, and God. I destroyed relationships and I was determined to leave everything, including my marriage. I told my husband this, fully expecting to be tossed out and to be "free" again. It was in this moment that I first experienced the true, unconditional love of Jesus, through my husband. Even as I was hurting my husband so deeply, he refused to let me leave. That is such a powerful statement to me. He refused to let me leave. He laid aside his pride and refused to give up on me. Forgiveness was immediate, and the healing began.

My husband thawed a tiny bit of my heart when he showed me the love of Jesus that day, but even he pales in comparison to the Source. Each and every day since, God has made my heart fuller, made my life richer, and restored those dark and broken innermost parts of me. He has shown me the truth about who I am in Him. Out of the pain and heartbreak, God has birthed ministries that I never could have imagined. Each and every day I feel the unconditional love of Jesus, but I will never forget that first day—the day that I tried to run away and God refused to let me leave."

– Alicia Crawford

A fish does not have to learn how swim. It is his nature to live in water. It is his natural environment. You never hear a tree groaning in an attempt to produce fruit. As a child of God you do not have to struggle to produce the fruit of love. You love because it is your nature.

Let it happen! By the love of God you are free to love and to live the pain free life! The world is waiting for you to love them.

DISCUSSION QUESTIONS

1. What is the greatest healing agent for emotional pain?

2. What is your definition of love?

3. What is the greatest gift that can be received?

4. How can a person know that they love God?

5. How does God know that we love Him?

6. Can a person love God and not love his brother?

7. Do you love yourself?

8. What are the spiritual benefits of adoption?

9. Will you allow the love of God to become your healing agent?

10. Who is going to teach you to love unconditionally?

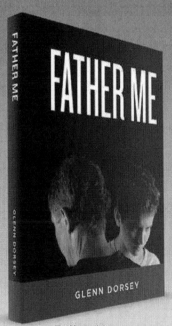

From author
GLENN DORSEY

Father Me

Presents the needs of a child that only a father can meet.
It also offers fathering skills to men that have not had a father,
or good relationship with their father. The struggles
experienced in a bad father-child relationship can be
healed by looking to God the Father as our model.

"He will turn the hearts of fathers to their children and
the hearts of children to their fathers." Malachi 4:6

Also Avaialbe in Ebook Format

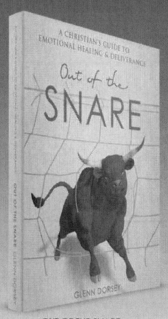

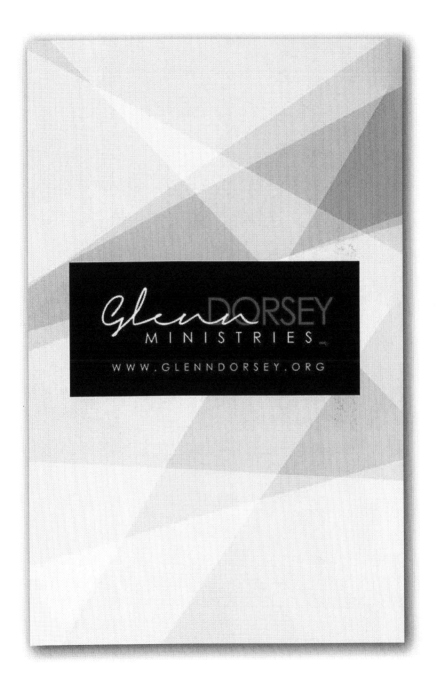

Made in the USA
Columbia, SC
17 June 2017